What people are saying about
At Home on the Kazakh Steppe

Kirkus Reviews:
... she writes engagingly ... a sharp-eyed journalist of the intriguing cultural separation between her world and Kazakhstan's. ... A worthwhile read for anyone with an interest in humanitarian work.

Leita Kaldi Davis, Peace Corps Worldwide Review
Thank goodness she decided to write this book, a delight for any reader.

Cynthia Werner, PhD, Chair, Dept of Anthropology, Texas A&M University
This heartfelt memoir provides a perfect introduction to many of the key cultural differences between Kazakhstan and the United States ... while reminding readers that it's never too late to follow your dreams....

Reeve Lindbergh, author, Under A Wing
... a lively, poignant, and delightful story about the adventures of a very energetic grandmother ... It is a pleasure to travel with her in this entertaining book.

Victoria Twead, New York Times bestselling author
Janet Givens' pen perfectly captures the mood and color of Kazakhstan, and her characters leap off the pages and into the arms of the reader. She set out to make a difference, and with this book, Janet Givens has done exactly that.

Shirley Showalter, author, former President, Goshen College
The writing is brisk, frequently humorous, and also philosophical without being ponderous. The excellent quotes about travel and perception show that the author has let the experience settle in the mind and heart, connecting it with all her prior learning in psychology and sociology.

Dr. Carlyn Syvanen, English Language Specialist, U.S. State Department
We learn about the world and our place in it through stories. And I really enjoyed reading Janet Givens' story of her two years in Kazakhstan for it reminded me that while we travel to learn about the world and others, in the process we learn more about ourselves.

Ian Mathie, author, Sorcerers and Orange Peel and others
Revealing, frustrating, and at times daunting, this is a fascinating book worth reading more than once, for each reading uncovers new interest. It has the benefit of being written by an author with extensive life experience, and the ability to distill complex ideas and feelings onto very readable prose. It deserves to be widely read.

Patrick Youngblood, author, The Coconut Chronicles
… memoir writing at its best—moving, informative and deeply insightful. The book paints a wonderful picture of life in Kazakhstan. … Very skillful indeed. … Buy this book—you won't regret it!

Sharon Lippincott, author, Adventures of a Chilihead
If social anthropology classes used textbooks like this, students would flock to register! ... It's the next best thing to being there!

Kathleen Pooler, author, Ever Faithful to His Lead
... descriptions of the people and the country are so rich in detail ... I am right there with her. ... Her writing is fluid and her voice is authentic and believable, laced with a delightful sense of humor ...

Ginger Moran, author, The Algebra of Snow
This is, quite simply, a marvelous book. Givens' telling of the story of their time in Kazakhstan is nothing short of a true education in life choices, today's Peace Corps, and the amazing, extraordinary people of Kazakhstan.

Linda Austin, author Cherry Blossoms in Twilight and others
The book holds a great message about the difficulties of world peace and understanding and how it really does begin with "me." Thank you, Janet, for teaching me about a country and culture I knew little about and for letting me grow with you.

RYCJ, Vine Voice
... a book I struggled to put down. Any reader who enjoys travel memoirs, or who is interested in Peace Corps work, will find this memoir a delightful true page-turner. Highly recommended.

At Home
on the
Kazakh Steppe

A Peace Corps Memoir

Janet Givens

At Home on the Kazakh Steppe

Fifth Edition

Published by Birch Tree Books, 2016

Also available in eBook and large print versions.

DEDICATED

to

Gulzhahan Zarubaevna Tazhitova
without whom this would have been
a very different story

and

Mikhail Sergeyevich Gorbachev
without whom this story never would have been

With grateful recognition of the work the Peace Corps continues to do around the world and in the hope that the work of peace and understanding they do so well will someday be unnecessary.

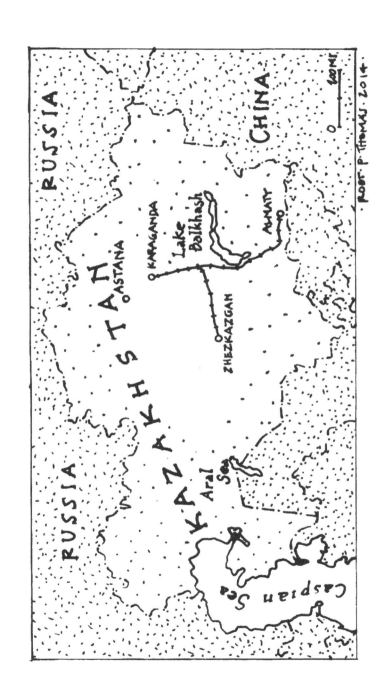

On that trip it was my good fortune to be wrong;
being mistaken is the essence of the traveler's tale.
Paul Theroux (1941 -)

PREFACE

Where does one begin? At the beginning, so it has been said. But just where does my Peace Corps memoir start?

While the story I tell here begins in August of 2004, when my husband and I finally arrived at our Peace Corps assigned work site, I like to think it actually began in the late 1970s, when I first heard that one could join the Peace Corps later in life. It was during the presidency of Jimmie Carter (1977-1981), and the American media was filled with the story of Miss Lillian, the president's mother, who had joined the Peace Corps some ten years earlier, at age 67, serving in India as a nurse.

Before I heard her story, I'd thought Peace Corps service was only for the young, recently graduated college student, one who had neither dependents nor career. I was thrilled to learn I was wrong.

By the late 1970s, I had both dependents and a career. But at least I knew that someday, perhaps when I was also in my 60s, I might still live out that old high school dream: to serve in the American Peace Corps. It would take me another thirty years to see my dream come true.

My story ends with Miss Lillian, too, in a way. During the summer following our return home, I found a copy of her book, *Away From Home: Letters to My Family*, in a used bookstore in Plains, Georgia. This was her Peace Corps story. Like Lillian Carter, I too had written letters home. During my two years in Kazakhstan, I'd sent seventeen email "updates" to no less than 108 people. I had my journals, too, and I had my memories. And so, in January 2007, I sat down at my computer and got to work.

Writing this book has allowed me to relive the highs and the lows of those two years in slow motion. I wrote first to understand my experience. Then I rewrote, and rewrote, so that I could share that experience with a broad array of readers.

My hope is that, in reading my story, you'll come to recognize two things.

The first is how vital it is that we humans learn to connect with one another over the artificial barriers of age, religion, gender, and culture. We *can* connect across these barriers. Indeed, as our world continues to get smaller, I believe we must.

The second is that opportunities to live out old dreams are all around us, if we can just see them. If ever you are presented with such an opportunity, I urge you to jump into it wholeheartedly. It is a gift not to be ignored.

Putting my story to paper has been, to pull from memoirist Anaïs Nin, a most delicious undertaking. She once said that memoirists get to live their life twice. "There is the living," she wrote, "and then there is the writing. There is the second tasting, the delayed reaction."

This is just one story; it's my story, of my experience, and the way I remember it. I encourage you to go to Kazakhstan and experience for yourself the gracious hospitality and warm embrace of the Kazakh people.

TABLE OF CONTENTS

PART I

Studying culture without experiencing culture shock is like practicing swimming without experiencing water.
Geert Hofstede (1928 -)

Chapter One
ARRIVAL

I was 55 when I stepped off that train into blinding sunshine and a new life in Kazakhstan, half a world away from the life I'd had in Philadelphia, Pennsylvania. Proud to finally be a Peace Corps volunteer, I was also determined to be successful, and for me that success would be simple: I'd make friends for America in the post 9/11 era.

To do this, I'd left behind a life I loved, given away a dog I adored, and abandoned the financial security that my work in Philadelphia had promised. I knew there was much I didn't yet know about Kazakhstan and her history, culture, and people, but with an MA in sociology, my more recent experience as a psychotherapist, and my husband by my side, I naively thought I had all I needed to succeed.

The day my husband Woody and I got off that train, we'd already been in Kazakhstan for nearly three months, been "trained" in the Russian language—he a bit better than I— learned about a few cultural differences we'd meet, and taken practice classes in how to teach English as a second language, our job for the next two years.

Our assigned destination was Zhezkazgan, a town once controlled by the now defunct Soviet Union and built with labor from the gulags to house the workers for the nearby copper mines. It wasn't much like my City of Brotherly Love, which had been laid out in a systematic grid pattern by the Quaker William Penn in the 17th century, and anchored by no less than five public parks. Nor was it at all like the tiny seaside town of Chincoteague, Virginia, where we'd lived temporarily after our Philadelphia house was sold, while waiting for our Peace Corps departure. In Zhezkazgan, there would be no weekly curbside garbage pickup, no opportunity to walk the beach, and no sound of migrating birds overhead. We'd be there for two years.

As I squinted in the glare of the sun, a young woman with bright red hair and denim overalls broke through the small crowd of locals that had come to welcome us and thrust a huge yellow bouquet into my hands.

"Welcome," she said in perfectly passable English, except that I didn't understand her. "These are for you."

Without thinking, I offered her one of the Russian phrases I'd committed to memory during training.

"*Meenya zavoot*, Janet. *Kak vas zavoot?*" (My name is Janet. What is yours?)

Why hadn't I said the more appropriate "*S'paceba*"? I wondered immediately. Or, the even more appropriate "Thank you," since she'd spoken to me in English?

At least I understood her answer: Natasha, the fourth Natasha I'd met since we'd been in Kazakhstan. Nevertheless, she seemed neither to notice nor care about my *faux pas*, and melded back into the welcoming crowd, which was chattering in a language I could not recognize.

About half a dozen women and nearly that many men were there to meet us, and I let my gaze fall on each face, wondering how well I would know these people before my time there was over. I smiled as I caught each eye. A few of the men had gone back into the train, directed there by the women whom I assumed were their wives, to fetch our luggage.

Our luggage. It had become an embarrassment to me over the three months since we'd arrived in the country. We simply had too much. I'd known it when we first flew out of Dulles

International Airport and had to pay $400 in overweight charges. I'd known it after our initial weekend in Almaty, Kazakhstan's former capital (and, in 2004, still its major city) when we had to leave a suitcase behind with the Peace Corps staff in order to fit into the car to ride to our first homestay.

And I knew it then, as the men handed suitcase after suitcase down the train's narrow steps into waiting arms on the platform below. These Kazakh men were descendants of nomads, I knew. Nomads, practically by definition, traveled light. And here we were, so American with our too-much stuff.

Two of the women in the group had been on the train with us. They were our "counterparts," local Kazakhstanis who worked where we would and were charged with helping us navigate the workplace. The previous week they had come to our training site in Almaty to participate in the Peace Corps' training for counterparts and to accompany us on the train to our permanent site. Having them with us, besides helping with tricky language challenges *en route*, had given us time to get to know each other.

Woody's counterpart, Aniya, seemed to evaporate into the crowd. But my counterpart, Gulzhahan, found her husband among the many welcomers and brought him over to introduce us.

Darkhan, no taller than my 5 feet 4 inches, had an easy smile and the best set of dimples I'd seen in a long time. Still, he towered over his tiny wife, whose shiny, black hair fit closely around her round, *café-au-lait* face. Gulzhahan and her husband looked Western in both their dress and their mannerisms. They could have passed for American Indians, albeit very short American Indians. But when Gulzhahan spoke, out came the Queen's English. I had found it disconcerting when I first met her. But now, after knowing her a full week, I noticed only how lively she was, happy. Our mutual nods and smiles and handshakes over, they too melded back into the crowd, now all suddenly on their cell phones.

Woody and I helped carry our luggage from the platform to the side of the nearby road—it was the least we could do, then we stood, waiting. I gave Woody a perplexed look, and he spoke (in Russian) to a woman who would turn out to be his boss at the University, to find out what was going on.

"We are looking for our taxis," Zamzagul answered in friendly, understandable English. "They should be here."

I was in no hurry. In fact, after our 36-hour train ride, I relished standing just a bit longer. Getting into a vehicle of any sort, no matter how short the next leg might be, was the last thing I wanted to do. I looked around, breathing in the cool late-summer air and appreciating that the ground beneath me no longer wobbled.

The small train station suggested that no one had held a paintbrush in a very long time. I paid it no mind, understanding that any country that would invite Peace Corps volunteers might not have the means to keep their infrastructure tiptop. My gaze drifted beyond the station to the oddest trees. Small orbs formed of spindly branches topped short but very fat trunks. With more shrubbery than a desert but not as green as a plain, the steppe, on which I now stood, was unlike anything I'd ever seen.

I was enveloped in magnificent sunshine, balmy breezes, a dozen or more of the world's friendliest people, and the bleakest landscape I'd ever known. And I smiled. I was right where I wanted to be.

⚜

If Kazakhstan were a dartboard, the city of Zhezkazgan would be within the bull's eye. I was standing 700 miles west of China and 600 miles south of Russia. Four hundred miles farther south lay the four other "Stans," lands of the ancient Uzbeks, Kyrgyz, Tajiks, and Turkmen, which, along with the land of the Kazakhs, constituted what was now sometimes called Central Asia, sometimes Eurasia.

The Caspian Sea was 750 miles away along her western border, and contained one of the largest pools of oil outside the Middle East. I'd read that it was pushing Kazakhstan, ready or not, onto the world's stage. But in August of 2004, when I first arrived in Zhezkazgan, nearly thirteen years after Kazakhstan's independence following the Soviet Union's collapse, I saw few signs of modernizing.

Soon enough, three late-model sedans with phone numbers painted on their sides pulled up: our missing taxis. Each had four doors and reminded me of the Chevy Nova my grandmother drove when I was in high school. In fact, they were Russian-made Ladas.

Woody and I got into the back seat of one these boxy sedans while an unidentified man hopped into the right front passenger seat, turned to look directly at us, and gave us a broad, happy smile. The rest of our welcoming committee went with our luggage, and we all headed into town on a paved but empty two-lane road. We were on our way to the home of our new "host family."

I kept my face turned to the window to see what I could of the town while we drove. It was an early Sunday morning and it appeared the town had not yet woken up. As we curved around a traffic circle, a billboard caught my eye.

The pudgy, pondering face of Kazakhstan's first and only president, Nursultan Nazarbayev, stared down at me, with 2030 in large, black numbers beside it. I'd seen these billboards during our training along the major roads into and out of Almaty.

I had once been an earnest PhD student in political science—ten years after I'd gotten my Masters in Sociology and ten years before I'd started my career as a Gestalt psychotherapist—and I relished the political intrigue of

Kazakhstan. And, though Peace Corps policy specifically forbade its volunteers to engage in any political activity, I could observe. And I could read.

The ninth largest country in the world and strategically placed between Russia and China, Kazakhstan had long ago become adept at playing what some call "The Great Game," as her monolithic neighbors vied for power and influence with Great Britain, over control of Asia. Now, President Nazarbayev had vowed to bring his country into the 21st century.

Nazarbayev was a big unknown to me in those early months. Depending on what I read or to whom I listened, he was either a power-loving dictator acting in his own self-interest within a sham of a democracy; a benevolent buffoon, catapulted into the limelight by forces he couldn't control; or a strong and capable leader and just what this young country needed. All of this fascinated me, and I looked forward to seeing how the politics of this still-young country would play out in real life.

The "2030" I'd seen referred to the president's long-range plan: what the country would look like by the year 2030. The plan set out a number of priorities in ten-year increments: to double the 2005 GNP by 2010; to create a five-year development plan by 2020; and to be "one of the 50 most competitive states" in the world by 2030.

Each time I saw one of these huge advertisements along the roadside in 2004, I wondered who'd be held accountable, twenty-six years hence, if the goals weren't met. Probably not the then sixty-three-year-old president.

My interest in Kazakhstan's politics waned as our caravan of taxis turned off the paved road and our car jostled over abundant potholes. We'd pulled into a residential area, and clusters of tall cement-block buildings rose from the sandy dirt; massive power-line towers stretched in one long row to our right. An empty, sparsely equipped playground stood in their shadow and bits of paper, from a row of dumpsters overflowing with garbage, danced in the wind.

"We're moving to the projects," I whispered to Woody, only half joking.

Raised poor, married to privilege, I felt up to meeting whatever challenge these next two years would bring.

Our taxi stopped amid a group of identical teal-colored cement block buildings, and parked on what might have been—long, long ago—a lawn. The apartments must have been painted blue once, but so many years before that the color had faded to teal green. And I couldn't help notice that the front door of our new building was missing.

Woody and I grabbed what we could from the pile of our bags that now rested on the ground, and followed the rest of our luggage, easily transported by the men of our welcoming party, into a dark, damp stairwell that smelled faintly of urine.

"Where there are men, the luggage is light," says a Kazakh proverb that Gulzhahan had taught me on the train. My "inner feminist" had privately scoffed at the time, but now I could see her point.

On the second floor landing, we passed an empty row of exposed mailboxes that reminded me I'd need to get a box at the post office if we wanted to get any mail. Still embedded within the concrete wall, the mailboxes' few remaining front panels hung askew. Of greater concern, however, was that nobody in our little party made any apologies for the disrepair. No one even seemed to notice.

Three flights up, on the top floor, we entered our new home. The Peace Corps policy was clear: we were to live with a host family for another six months. Designed to help ease our adjustment to local life, it was, I thought, a good way to meet the local people. One of my hopes was that these local people— who'd never met an American before—would like me. And through me, they would like America. Living with a host family seemed to be an easy route to that goal.

Woody, though, did not relish the requisite formality, as he put it, of living like guests in a stranger's home. Still, he was willing to do anything to get closer to his goal: to teach English. Woody and I approached our Peace Corps adventure in different ways, and our attitude about the "host family" requirement was just one example. I would discover many more over the next few months.

Shoes filled the hall as the members of our entourage moved inside. Though we'd been in Kazakhstan nearly three months by then, the shoes-off-at-the-door ritual still felt new and it always took thought. The locals slipped theirs off easily, often without breaking stride, while ours had to be untied, unbuckled, or unVelcroed, and generally without a chair on which to sit.

My Teva sandals were off before Woody's sneakers, and I walked with bare feet into the spacious and clean but sparsely furnished apartment. I found the women from our welcome committee busy in the kitchen.

My yellow bouquet from the train station had found its way into a jar of water, and I stood watching as the women bustled about as though they lived there. I knew they didn't.

According to the information sheet our Peace Corps trainers had given us, this was home to three people: our new "host parents" and their eighteen-month-old son. But I had no idea who they were or if they were even there. No one had introduced us and I hadn't seen a toddler.

Woody passed behind me and I followed him into what someone had indicated was "our room." We set the baggage we were carrying down amid the pile of our bags already there and looked around.

Furnished only with a tall, narrow wardrobe along the wall next to the door and a small wooden table pressed against another wall, the room was essentially empty. I saw no dresser, no chairs and, more importantly, no bed.

Curious, I thought, and smiled to myself. But sleep was hours away. We had lots of time to deal with a missing bed. First we would eat. We would always eat first.

Woody and I left the bedroom and drifted back toward the living room. While he went in and sat down, I stopped and watched the women at work in the kitchen. "Well-oiled machine" came to mind. There was no bumping into each other, no questioning even. Each one had a job to do and was bustling about doing it, all under a steady hum of conversation and laughter.

My instinct was to ask if I might help. But I already knew better. Instead, I turned to catch up with Woody in the living room where the husbands were moving tables together and collecting chairs. I joined him on the sofa safely out of the way. As the honored guests, Woody and I were actually not allowed to help. And, on this day, I was grateful.

"Honored guest" is an understatement. In Kazakhstan, a guest is a gift from God. Really, it's not a metaphor. And at that moment, I loved the custom. Tired from our extended train trip and overwhelmed at all the sudden activity around me, I relished the opportunity to just relax next to my husband and watch the others.

Soon, chairs appeared on three sides of a long table covered with food. Flower-bearing, denim-clad, red-haired Natasha sat next to me on the arm of the sofa. And the feasting began.

Food is such a traditional way of welcoming guests anywhere. In Kazakhstan quantity is important. How full the tabletop is reflects the bounty of the family, and they would use all the food available for the week to fill it if necessary.

The table that day held plates of cold sausages, bread, cheese, salads, and *chai* (tea). There would always be *chai* and the white sugar to go in it, or sometimes honey, or, more often, jam. There were also hard candies and pastries of different shapes and sizes. Of all the things we'd given up to be there, the low-carb diet we'd followed for the previous three years was surely the easiest. We dove in.

The chatter during the meal was in Kazakh, for which I was oddly grateful. If everyone had been speaking English, I'd have felt compelled to participate; they'd be speaking for, if not to us. If they'd been speaking Russian, I'd have felt obliged to attend to the conversation, too, and at least attempt to identify an occasional word; I was too tired for that. But they spoke Kazakh and I was off the hook. The Peace Corps had offered us just twenty hours of Kazakh language lessons over the same weeks we'd had 360 hours of Russian. Nobody expected us to speak it, at least not yet.

When the meal was finally over, sometime later, the women moved to the kitchen to clean up and I stayed seated with Woody and the other men at the table, strangely relieved that to offer assistance at this point would be insulting. I wanted more than anything to climb onto my bed and nap or, more to the point, to hibernate. Our bed—at least the frame—had arrived during the meal, carried in by three hefty and very young men, and it was calling to me.

Woody, I noticed, was engaging with the men in Russian. Already fluent in Dutch, French, and German, he'd been eager to add Russian to the list and so far, he was on track. I envied his facility with language but my exhaustion left me disconnected from my surroundings, from the men at the table, and even from my husband, a feeling I hadn't experienced for a very long time.

This was far from the life I'd known, and not only geographically. In the ten years I'd known Woody, we'd reveled in how connected we always felt, even when we disagreed. That abiding sense of connection—our manifest destiny—would keep us together, no matter what obstacle fell before us. At least that's what I'd believed when I'd married him four years earlier.

It's what I still believed as I sat there, numb, and very, very sleepy, while all around me swirled a bevy of activity.

Chapter Two
THE DECISION

The Peace Corps was five years old when I graduated high school. I'd known of its existence since its founding in 1961, and had thought it a most exciting adventure, something I'd surely love to do one day.

When I finished my bachelor's degree and had the two qualifications then needed to join—American citizenship and a college education—the Peace Corps was still young, not yet ten. But by the time I finally lived that adventure, it would be nearing its fiftieth year. And I'd be well past mine.

It's not that I didn't want to join when all my college friends were talking up their applications and future plans in Thailand, or Ethiopia, or India. My problem was that I believed I'd be rejected.

Why bother to try, if you're just going to fail? That was my motto then.

I was smart, healthy, and committed to the principles that guided the Peace Corps. But I also had a secret I'd been trying to hide. I stuttered. And because I stuttered, I couldn't imagine that they'd want me.

Until I was in my forties, stuttering was paramount in nearly every decision of my life, each one geared to keeping my stuttering hidden.

I went to great lengths to avoid certain sounds, subjects, and situations. If a word began with a sound that was going to "get stuck," I'd simply substitute a different word, less concerned with the oddness of my resulting sentence. The answers I gave when called upon in school, the food I ordered in restaurants, the letters I could see at the optometrist, all fell victim at one time or another to my determination to keep my stuttering from showing.

I stayed away from conversations in which I might need to persuade, convince, or argue; I found any of these turned quickly into exposure filled with shame and humiliation. I also steered clear of microphones, telephones, and spotlights of any sort. But even with so much effort, my stuttering did occasionally erupt. How could I possibly serve in the Peace Corps with such a disability constantly hovering?

Instead of serving my country, I got married and moved from New York City to Cleveland, Ohio. Within six months, I'd gone from life as an anti-war demonstrating sociology student at New York University in Greenwich Village, New York to being the suburban Ohio housewife of a Republican businessman. I felt safe, secure; I valued stability.

Before long, I was a stay-at-home mom, baking bread and hanging wallpaper in our brand-new four-bedroom home. But as our two sons grew, a lupus misdiagnosis propelled me into graduate school for the Masters in sociology I'd long wanted. Then, a number of increasingly challenging jobs in fund-raising followed.

For twenty-three years we lived a comfortable life, always slightly beyond our means, as was the norm in the Cleveland suburb we called home. But regardless of the many creature comforts I enjoyed, I was lonely. Despite the delight I felt at the birth of each of my boys, and my determination to be the best mother I could be, I remained unsettled. I longed for companionship, for conversations that lasted more than two sentences with an increasingly distant and taciturn husband.

Conversation is what brought Woody and me together. We'd met on the Internet in 1993, long before chat rooms and computer-dating services existed. Woody's professional focus as professor of speech communication was stuttering and, in that capacity he'd started an email listserv out of Temple University that brought stutterers together from around the world. I joined as part of a newly adopted quest to learn about stuttering.

After years of not wanting to read or hear or think about stuttering, I'd emerged from my metaphorical stuttering closet and was eagerly soaking up all I could about both stuttering in general and my stuttering in particular. That led me to Woody.

Back then, there were no links to open, no websites to visit, no photo exchanges, no chat rooms, and no text messaging. There was instead a comfortable dialogue about our lives, past and current. For me, right then, there could have been no better aphrodisiac than a man listening to my every word, and hearing me, even if it was through a computer monitor.

I'd write at night, after dinner, while my husband watched television and my remaining still-at-home son was off into his own world of late-adolescent exploration. Woody would write early in the morning, before his wife and his also-seventeen-year-old son had awakened. Soon enough I came to look forward to those brief exchanges with an unexpected sense of excitement.

Six weeks later, when I found myself in his neighborhood on my way home from a college reunion, I asked to meet. He was Greek-god handsome, broad-shouldered, and had a full crop of white hair and a beard. Our morning coffee lasted through lunch, and to say we enjoyed our visit is an understatement. But he was a professor at Temple University in Philadelphia, and the lives we believed we were committed to were 400 miles apart.

Back home in Ohio, I continued my participation in the listserv and the email correspondence with Woody. I didn't think about any future we might have, but I did know he had awakened in me the passion and romance I'd forgotten existed—and I wanted more.

From the therapy that had helped me emerge from my closet of shame, and from countless 12-Step meetings over nearly three years, I'd learned to listen to—call it what you will—my gut, my body, or my internal voice. To do that, honesty with myself was essential. I wanted to set about making room for romance in my life in an open, honest way. With integrity. My relationship with Woody, whatever it might become, had to be open and transparent. Of that I was sure.

As fall moved into winter, my long-overdue divorce was finally underway, and I began a nationwide search for employment. Though my divorce would take a few years to finalize, I accepted a job offer in fundraising for the University of Pennsylvania. That it was in Woody's backyard, I took as an omen.

I moved to Philadelphia in March of 1994 and rented a room in Woody's house for a few weeks while I found an apartment. That he was newly single made life fun as, over the next few years, I experimented with and enjoyed a newfound Mary-Tyler-Moore-type single life, and Woody and I got to know each other better.

When he was asked in 1995 to write a new textbook on stuttering, Woody asked me to join him as second author. It was a collaboration between the professional and the stutterer, a partnership that led to our offering workshops for stutterers (and the professionals who treated them) on three continents.

Through it all he courted, wooed, and won me with elegant dinners, romantic vacations, frequent movies, and all the extensive and heartfelt conversations I wanted. My inner voice, my gut, kept pushing me toward him rather than away. And when I listened to it, my inner voice—that gut feeling deep in the core of my solar plexus—told me my truth. It hadn't always been so, certainly. But by age 47 I'd learned to slow down and listen to myself.

In 1996, with my divorce complete, I bought a house on Philadelphia's west side, within walking distance of my job at the university. A year later, Woody moved in, and six years to the day after we'd first spoken in person, we married.

For the next two years, I reveled in the contented, happy, and as a result, serene life I had created. Then Woody threw a pebble into my still waters, creating ripples that would carry me all the way to Kazakhstan.

It happened on our drive home from a glorious three-day weekend in late May—Memorial Day 2002—at a little cabin we owned on Chincoteague Island, Virginia. Good friends from my earlier life in Ohio had met us there, towing their shallow draft sailboat behind them. The foreign students, who rented rooms on our third floor, rented a car and drove down from Philadelphia to join us. We'd kept busy on the water and on land, and had a perfect weekend as we laughed, ate, and played. I expected we'd have many more. But we never had another.

On the drive home, out of the blue, Woody let the pebble drop.

"We should go in the Peace Corps," he said as we drove north, back to our Philadelphia life.

I just stared at him. Then I snickered; or maybe it was a guffaw. The idea was so ludicrous to me that I discounted it completely. We'd been renovating our little beach house for nearly two years and now, finally, we could relax and enjoy the fact that we had balmy breezes and salty sea air seducing us out of the city. *How could he even think I'd be willing to give this up?*

I'd also been building a new career over the preceding five years—a career I loved. For the first time in my adult life, I wasn't looking for something else. *How could he not know that?*

I wasn't about to climb up onto another high dive, I told myself, never mind jump. Then he reminded me that the idea of our joining the Peace Corps had first come from me.

"Lillian Carter joined the Peace Corps when she was in her 60s," I'd said to him on one of our early dates, telling him of my high school dream. And he'd agreed that he'd also like to do that someday, in his 60s. But that conversation had been before we

19

had a future, long before I'd found such contentment with my life.

The ensuing weeks were filled with Woody's casual references to the Peace Corps. His enthusiasm was hard to ignore. He was, in fact, the most excited I'd seen him since he'd retired from the University the year before.

He'd been bored, and not a little disappointed that his influence in the field of speech pathology, and the research and treatment of stuttering that he'd long committed himself to, had waned with his retirement. He'd looked into teaching English as a Second Language, only to find he'd need additional training leading to certification. Being in the Peace Corps, he discovered, would offer him a chance to teach English, a dream he'd had since his own high school years. And, as a bonus, he would add yet another foreign language to his list.

"Have you checked out the Peace Corps web site?" he'd ask me every now and again during those weeks. He cajoled me with, "We can choose our region." And, knowing I'd long wanted to see Tahiti, he added, "They have placements in the South Pacific."

Finally, to shut him up, I visited the www.peacecorps.gov site, and was quickly hooked back into the dream I'd dismissed earlier in my life when I thought I was not good enough.

Going into the Peace Corp was a classically romantic idea. It would be even more romantic to go in now, I thought, as a newly married, older couple, "abandoning worldly possessions in pursuit of loftier goals."

In all seriousness, this was not that long after 9/11, and I did want to serve my country. I calculated that if I could do so in the South Pacific, so much the better. *Tonga, Kiribati, or Vanuatu*—where the Peace Corps had programs—*here I come.*

My enthusiasm was tempered, though, by what I'd have to give up, and the anticipated sacrifices felt enormous. It was more than just things, though they were considerable. Dave, my older son, had recently married a Cincinnati, Ohio girl, and Jon's Ohio wedding would occur the following October. With Jon's marriage, I'd inherit my first grandchild, three-year-old Mikah, whom I already adored. Surely, we couldn't leave before the wedding.

What would I do with my clients, my psychotherapy practice? I loved my new identity as a Gestalt psychotherapist. The work I did was built on the premise that the relationship between therapist and client is critical to the process. How would I end those relationships?

What would we do with our pets? We had a stray street cat, Molly, that we'd adopted the previous year, and we had our dog, a rescued greyhound named Merlin that we loved.

Our material possessions were not insignificant either. *What would we do with our two homes?* We could easily rent the Chincoteague home, since it was in a tourist area. But the Philadelphia home I owned was a symbol of my independence, my personal accomplishment. Before I moved in I'd renovated it and put in the best master bathroom a woman could have, complete with French bidet and a six-foot long claw-foot tub. I loved that bathtub. I couldn't leave it standing empty for two years. *Could I rent the house? Should I sell it?*

It was hard to wrap my mind around all the decisions that I would have to make in order to join the Peace Corps at this stage of my life. But once I made the decision to join, I knew that I would simply cross each bridge as I came to it. I would take this all one day at a time. Literally.

So, at age fifty-three, I applied to the Peace Corps and to its romantic American idea that if we can just get to know people as people, prejudice and fear will fade away. That was certainly the dream in 1960 when presidential candidate John F. Kennedy first proposed a two-year overseas commitment to a group of idealistic college students in Ann Arbor, Michigan. And it was still the dream a year later when, through executive order, President Kennedy signed the Peace Corps into reality.

Two years after our initial interview with a Peace Corps recruiter, I finally stepped off the train in the town of Zhezkazgan and into that blinding sunshine.

My life had wended its way from lonely only child of the 1950s and '60s to lonely Stepford Wife in the 1970s and '80s. Then, in the 1990s, I'd had my awakening, the inevitable divorce, and a new life of such satisfaction and reward I often asked friends to pinch me.

Now, as a new millennium dawned, I found myself about to give up that life too, and to jump off an unexpected high dive into a great unknown. And I was ready.

When I'd filled out my online application, I told myself that, if accepted, I'd live the Peace Corps experience to its fullest. I'd live within the means that Peace ocrps set for us, stay for the full twenty-seven-month commitment, come to know the locals, and maybe even find a girlfriend or two. More importantly, the I encountered would like me. And as they liked me, they'd like my country, the country I now represented. I'd be one of the Peace Corps success stories.

As Woody put it to a newspaper reporter shortly before we left, we were going to "make friends for America." If we did, then, and only then, would I know it was worth all I'd given up.

Chapter Three
NEW BEGINNINGS

Our new host "parents" were Yergali, 29, and his wife, Symbat, 23. Our new "brother" was 18-month-old Yeerasul. We knew these basics from our Peace Corps information sheet. What the sheet didn't tell us was that Yergali and Symbat spoke Kazakh, and, while they knew Russian, they didn't plan to speak it in their home.

The father, Yergali, looked fit, muscular even, though of slight build. He moved around the house in quick, long strides. He had a wide smile that occasionally lit up an otherwise stern face, but not nearly enough. His hair was chopped short and always looked tousled. Symbat, his young wife, couldn't have been more different.

"Yergali strides, but Symbat glides," I told Woody after our first day with them.

Symbat's bare feet carried her tall, thin frame silently as she moved from room to room. She had a perfectly proportioned face with porcelain skin, and I thought her beautiful. Her demeanor was somber, even sad. Her shoulders were stooped, as though she carried a burden we couldn't see. I also thought her fragile.

Eighteen-month old Yeerasul was not yet walking or talking. He smiled appropriately and showed typical toddler curiosity in the world around him, but stick-thin legs couldn't hold him up and his head was visibly larger than average. We never knew why.

He was also not potty trained and often didn't wear diapers, though diapers were available. Symbat bought one on a walk we took on our second evening. Yes, one diaper. The storeowner had opened a package of Huggies on the shelf behind his counter and sold her one, at three times the cost of a bus ride. But at home, Yeerasul continued to crawl through the house, dragging his flaccid legs behind him, with nothing beneath his big smile but a T-shirt.

Symbat, Yergali, and Yeerasul slept in the back room of the four-room apartment, while Woody and I used the front bedroom, next to the kitchen. We had two double-casement south-facing windows that pushed open to let in an infrequent breeze. There were no screens. The windowsills were wide enough to accommodate my accumulating books and papers from training, and I felt quite organized placing them there our first night.

Our mattress was makeshift from a collection of thin, wool blankets, more than I'd ever seen in any single household. Each had a different color and pattern and was so heavy I couldn't lift more than one at a time. The massive wardrobe was in two parts, with shelves behind double doors on the top half and two deep drawers below. With no place to hang our clothes, we folded everything to put on a shelf or in a drawer. We created bedside tables using our two rolling suitcases turned on their sides. I covered mine with my raincoat, the only use the coat would get in that dry climate.

Woody and I were silent as we unpacked our belongings, attempting to make our room as homey as we could that first evening. Personally I felt a certain pride that, as fledgling Peace Corps volunteers, this was exactly as it was supposed to be. I remembered my commitment to live as the locals lived, and I held out hope that perhaps Symbat would become that friend I was looking for. But I had no clue how Woody felt. I was lost in my own world.

Two tiny closets in between the two bedrooms held a flush toilet in one and a small sink and bathtub in the other. Woody's body relaxed visibly when he saw the toilet, and he gave a grateful sigh. I understood. During our training, we'd lived in the home of a local Turkish couple and their four teenagers. They had a squat toilet in the backyard outhouse, and Woody had grown weary of sitting on its splintery wooden floor, his creative adjustment after discovering he had trouble squatting.

But I'd arrived with an outhouse advantage. My grandmother, on our regular excursions into New York City from my home in northern New Jersey, had taught me how to squat, holding my little-girl panties out in front of me and bending forward ever so slightly. I'd developed good thigh muscles as a result and could hold my position as long as needed. But aiming, I discovered, was now a problem. After two children, I'd developed a clear right hook. I too would be grateful to sit.

The kitchen was the brightest room by far. The sun shone in through the lone south-facing window, bouncing off the white walls, white refrigerator, white stove, and white sink. With no kitchen calendar, clock, or photos of—or "artwork" from— little Yeerasul covering the refrigerator, there was nothing to break up the expanse of white. I thought of the old movie, *A Clockwork Orange*, as I sat that first morning with my *chai* before getting dressed.

Woody and I tried to put on a brave front during our first weeks in Zhezkazgan, but we were miserable. If we weren't silently maintaining our stiff upper lips about our living conditions, we were arguing.

I actually liked the fact that we could argue. I'd never had a decent argument with my first husband, which I now understood was a function of how insecure I'd felt in the marriage. With Woody, I felt secure enough to fight with him. To me, that was a good thing, for the most part.

We'd had our first Peace Corps disagreement during our first night on the train. We'd stopped at a particularly lively station at two in the morning, and I was eager to get off and explore. It appeared we'd be there for some time. But Woody had balked, asking me not to get off; he was afraid the train would leave without me.

Although I eventually deferred to his wish, I'd taken note that he was different in this new country. Somehow, he was not the fearless, adventuresome man with whom I'd traveled around the world over the previous nine years.

Our second fight hit closer to home, and threatened one of the main goals I'd had in joining the Peace Corps. Woody wanted us to buy cell phones once we were in Zhezkazgan. I didn't. Cell phones, to me, seemed inconsistent with the Peace Corps' mandate to "live at the level of the local colleagues."

We skirted around the topic for a while. Finally, the day after that first disagreement, still on the train to Zhezkazgan, he made his case.

"They'll help us stay in touch," he argued, though his voice never once was raised. Woody rarely raises his voice; he's not as enamored with arguments as I am. "You'll be at the college; I'll be at the university. Landlines won't be so easy to find when we're at work."

"You don't know that," I snapped, and turned away from him, furious that he was pulling factoids out of thin air to suit himself.

I always felt at a disadvantage when we argued. Perhaps because of my stuttering and years of staying out of conversations in which I might wind up disagreeing or needing to persuade, I'd never had a chance to practice.

"Maybe not, but everyone here has them," Woody countered.

This I couldn't argue with. Everyone we'd met so far did have one. It was also true that our Peace Corps jobs would put us on different sides of town. But still, I couldn't see what problem either of us might have for which we'd need cell phones.

"If an emergency comes up, I'll ask Gulzhahan to help me," I countered.

She at least knew the town and the language.

All Woody wanted to do was to stay in touch with me, as he had said at the start. But I'd missed that part of his argument.

"We don't get enough money to pay for them," I argued.

We'd get 31,000 *tenge* (about $230) each month from the Peace Corps to cover our housing, travel, and other expenses. Most of that would go to pay our rent, and I had no idea how expensive life in Zhezkazgan would be. I wanted first to get a handle on the budget I'd be overseeing. I thought my rational argument would end the discussion. It didn't.

"We'll take it out of the home account," Woody responded. "We have our bank cards from home, after all."

We did. I'd brought them to use during our summer vacation, not to circumvent the Peace Corps' budget.

"I was looking forward to living within the budget set by the Peace Corps," I pleaded, and I meant it.

I'd spent most of my adult life with two men, neither of whom followed a budget. With my first husband, our open-ended home equity loan had absorbed our financial indiscretions, to an eventual financial crisis. Woody had had the remains of a small inheritance when we first met, and he dipped into it whenever the spirit moved. Yes, neither husband had put much stock in budgets.

I'd had a budget when I lived alone those few years in Philadelphia. And my single mother had had one while I was growing up. Our housing expenses never exceeded twenty-five percent of her monthly income; our food was measured in cost per bag. I still remember the day she proudly averaged $10 a bag.

I wanted to know that Woody and I could stick to a budget. I suddenly realized that seeing myself—and Woody—live within our income had been an expectation of mine, even before I'd left. And I had worked so hard to set each expectation aside as quickly as it arose.

An enormous sense of disappointment built within me as I realized I was going to lose this particular battle. But I gave it one more go.

"I feel like we'd be cheating."

"Cheating? No way. The Peace Corps has no rules against buying cell phones."

"No, not cheating them; cheating ourselves." Sadness settled on my shoulders.

"How?"

"Out of the proper Peace Corps experience," I said, imagining Peace Corps volunteers of the sixties mucking about in the mud, digging latrines, an image far removed from our Peace Corps reality.

We Calvinists get our sense of virtue from suffering and living poor. This, alone, held some surprising appeal. Woody, however, was not saddled with the same Puritan-Calvinist baggage from his youth that I was. He saw no inherent value in suffering. He wanted us to have cell phones. There was no rule against it and we could afford them if we used our own money.

As I would often do, I relented.

There were also challenges that Woody and I would face together. And one that all Peace Corps volunteers faced, no matter where they lived: the tap water was undrinkable.

During training, we'd filled our water bottles from the classroom water coolers and we never really thought about it. Now, at our permanent site, there was no such convenience. We'd have to use the electric distiller that the Peace Corps had given us. It wasn't so much the bacteria that created the problem; boiling could have taken care of that. It was the heavy metals we were trying to avoid. And although the Peace Corps was quick to tell us that "studies showed that two years of consuming heavy metals wasn't enough time to leave any permanent damage in an adult," they also told us to peel our fruit before eating. "Always."

I set up the distiller on the floor of our bedroom and ran it during the night. The three liters it held took six hours to distill. In the morning I filled our water bottles with the cleaned water, rinsed out the dark brown sludge that collected at the bottom, and refilled it from the kitchen faucet, ready to turn on again that night. This quickly became part of my evening routine.

Another challenge we shared was our frustration with Symbat and Yergali. The most obvious one was the language barrier. Our language training had been Russian, the *lingua franca* throughout the land, but not in our new home. When we used the Russian we'd learned, they looked at us like they didn't understand, though we knew they spoke Russian. During Soviet times, everyone spoke Russian.

Symbat had studied English in school and wanted to practice English words with us and that was fine. But Yergali wanted us to learn Kazakh. He'd write down Kazakh words on a pad of paper and next to them, since he knew no English, the Russian equivalents. It could have been Mandarin, to me.

At an early "lesson," during which Woody had quietly retired to our bedroom, I recognized enough Russian words to deduce he wanted to teach me the days of the week and seasons of the year. My head was already spinning from trying to remember the Russian I'd been taught over the previous three months. I was starting to lose it, having no chance to speak it.

I was annoyed with the Peace Corps for placing us in a Kazakh-speaking home when they'd trained us in the Russian language. Fairly or not, I was also mad at Woody, the Linguaphile, for not making the problem go away. Besides, it had been his idea to leave his—our—dictionary with our first host family in Almaty as a gift. The more I thought about it, the angrier I got.

Stifling angry feelings was not the best way to build a relationship with our new family.

Chapter Four
LIFE IN ZHEZKAZGAN

The day after we arrived, we got to see the town. Woody had arranged with Zamzagul, his new boss at the university, and her husband, Nariman, to help us buy those cell phones I so didn't want. They met us at the apartment about ten o'clock that morning.

Zamzagul and Nariman were the opposite of the fabled Jack Sprat (who could eat no fat) and his wife (who could eat no lean).

Nariman was heavyset and jovial. I thought he'd make a good Santa Claus at a Christmas party, but assumed it unlikely in this largely Muslim country. I was mistaken, however; come Christmas, Santa was everywhere. Even Woody would get his own Santa suit so he could play one at his university.

Zamzagul, at less than ninety pounds, had a directness that I enjoyed. When our Kazakhstani trainers had told us the locals tended toward "indirect communication," I took it as a euphemism for "beating around the bush." Zamzagul didn't beat around the bush; in fact, she could be downright bossy, an important trait in a department director, I imagined.

Once they'd finished taking off their shoes and greeting Symbat in the local language, they turned their attention to us.

"Good morning," we said all around in English. Even Nariman.

Woody greeted him in the extended two-handed manner he'd learned during training, saying the requisite "*As Salaam Aleichem.*" My husband loved opportunities to use this traditional male-only Arabic greeting used among Muslims, executing his flawless pronunciation.

We headed into town on foot, in search of the cell phones I disdained. It was a good jaunt across the pot-holed, dust-covered expanse that connected the former lawn to the road, then a half dozen blocks up Abai *Ulitza* (Street), to Nekrasova *Ulitza*, and finally another five or six blocks. The sidewalks became crowded as we neared the shopping district, and the passing cars sprayed a fine powder in their wake.

"It's quite a beige town," I said to Woody as we meandered down the sidewalk. Buildings, sidewalks, streets—everywhere I looked, I saw faded, dirty beige.

"The dogs are shaped like the trees," he responded, nodding toward a short-legged, smallish canine snuffling the curb just a few feet away. "Must have to do with adapting to the cold."

We hadn't seen them often, but the dogs we did see had very short legs and chunky bodies. They roamed loose, scrounging what they could.

"I was afraid I'd feel sorry for the dogs, you know?" I said. "Maybe want to adopt one. But so far, we're safe."

Pets as I knew them did not exist in Kazakh families. Dogs and cats, I'd read, were feral. They carried diseases and they stayed outside, even in the subzero winters. As I looked at the skinny, oddly shaped forager Woody had pointed out, I had no desire to make friends with him. But it was less the scrounging-looking mutt than my still-fresh anguish over losing Merlin that quenched any desire for another dog.

Two weeks before we'd left, the foster family we'd placed him with had backed out and the new family we'd found would only take him if we agreed to leave him with them permanently. My decision to let him go had broken my heart and left me sobbing on and off for two days. I even questioned my decision to go into the Peace Corps. No; I wasn't ready to replace him.

Nariman knew just where we should look for our phones. And he knew many other places he wanted to show us, too. Within our first three hours, I'd bought a detailed book of Zhezkazgan street maps in a small store that sold paper products, made a long-overdue appointment for two days hence at a hair salon he knew about, met countless friends of theirs and stopped to watch them chat on the sidewalk, and wandered into a dozen stores within a six-block radius to check out their cell phone offerings. But we still hadn't bought any phones. Exhausted, we broke for lunch at a small café filled with cigarette smoke.

"In America," I told Zamzagul, who'd been asking questions about my country as we shopped, "we've passed laws to prevent people smoking in restaurants."

She laughed. "That would never happen here."

Pity, I thought. And so European.

After lunch, we headed across the street to our final store, where Woody and Nariman settled on two matching phones at 11,000 *tenge* (about $80) each. Now that we knew how much, we needed to get the money.

For that we walked back to a cash machine near the post office and withdrew 30,000 *tenge* (about $200) from our home account. This would be enough, we thought, to buy two phones.

"As easy as that," I reported aloud.

My initial surprise to find such a modern convenience as an automated teller machine in the "middle of nowhere" was quickly followed by shock at my spurt of conceit. I'd assumed my "inner sociologist" wouldn't fall for such ethnocentric judgments. It would take me a few months to appreciate just how much the stress of all the "newness" was affecting my judgment.

We returned to the store to buy the phones, only to learn we had to buy SIM cards separately, and 30,000 *tenge* wasn't enough. So, Woody bought his phone and SIM card, and Zamzagul decided she and I would return the next day, after I made another withdrawal from our home account.

Walking out of the store, I smiled at the irony of this new glitch. In the spirit of the Peace Corps, I'd determined to try on a different way of being in the world, assuming it would be poor and uncomfortable. But that different way of being appeared to be more one of rolling with the punches. I was more than happy to live one more day without a cell phone.

I had another opportunity to roll with the punches the next morning when Zamzagul called. She and Woody were beckoned to their university to meet the rector, and she needed to cancel our jaunt. I phoned Gulzhahan right away.

"Can you take me to buy a cell phone?" I asked.

Technically, Gulzhahan's job as counterpart was confined to our workplace. But we had developed an easy, friendly rapport both during the weeklong counterpart conference in Almaty where we'd done our training and then on the two-day train trip to Zhezkazgan. I looked forward to spending time with her and getting to know her better. We agreed to meet at the store where the trek with Zamzagul had ended.

When she arrived, we discovered that the phone Woody had bought had increased dramatically in price. Overnight.

With a simple, "Do not worry," Gulzhahan led me to a new store where we found a little red phone, with SIM card, for only 8,000 *tenge* ($50).

And when she and I exchanged phone numbers, a mere forty-five minutes later, I was actually glad I had a phone. If it takes a cell phone to live like the locals, I decided, I was all for it.

As we walked toward the bus stop, Gulzhahan and I exchanged stories. I already knew she was 29, younger than my firstborn and only one year older than my second one; she was the youngest of five siblings.

"How long have you wanted to be an English teacher?" I asked as we walked.

"I planned to be German teacher," she said, laughing as she maneuvered gingerly around an open pothole in the sidewalk. "But there was no work."

Like most Kazakhstani English teachers that I would meet, by the time Gulzhahan had graduated, just a few years after independence, there were more opportunities to teach English than German.

"So I became an English teacher." She made it sound so easy. "I worked at the school in my village, then at the college."

She'd been teaching English for eight years by then. Still, she wanted to improve her craft. That's why she'd eagerly taken the volunteer post of Peace Corps counterpart. I knew she cared about being a good teacher, like her father, now "on his pension" after teaching world history at the local secondary school.

"I want to learn new teaching techniques," she'd told me the week we first met. And now, as we walked the few blocks to the bus stop, she said it again, adding that she wanted the other teachers at the college to learn them, too. I admired the way she saw the bigger picture, including her colleagues at a time when her own advancement might have been her only focus.

"I want to learn new teaching techniques, too," I had said, smiling at the irony of being the purported "expert," yet feeling quite unprepared.

She'd laughed, thinking I was joking. I hadn't been. Up to this point in my life, I'd taught only two semesters of American National Government while I was a PhD student back in the early 1990s. I hadn't felt particularly effective, either. Back then, standing in front of a compulsory early-morning class of college freshmen and sophomores, my goal had been to keep my stutter under control. And what energy I had was further sapped by the drama unfolding around me at home, where my suburban nuclear family was imploding.

My adolescent son had begun doing what first-born adolescent sons tend to do—act out—something for which neither his father nor I were prepared. One year after hauling the family into therapy, I left graduate school for good and got myself into therapy, too. I hadn't taught since.

But things were different now. And I was different. Committed to my own growth, both emotionally and spiritually, I saw teaching in the Peace Corps as a chance at a do-over for me. Life doesn't always give us such opportunities, and I was grateful I was getting one. Yes, I was eager to learn all I could.

When Gulzhahan and I reached the bus stop, we hugged good-bye. But the day was so pleasant, I decided to walk home, ready to show Woody my new red cell phone and exchange numbers.

⬥⬥⬥

My fifty-sixth birthday fell three days after we arrived in Zhezkazgan. In Kazakhstan, where the birthday honoree hosts a big party in her home and does all the work herself, I was concerned this would cause extra work for Symbat.

So I talked to Gulzhahan, who suggested that I host my party at a local restaurant. Through her, I invited almost everyone we then knew in Zhezkazgan: Gulzhahan and Darkhan, Zamzagul and Nariman, Woody's counterpart Aniya and her adult daughter, and Symbat and Yergali. All gave a resounding "Yes," so I set about getting ready.

At 11am on August 25th, my birthday, I was face down over a beauty salon sink having what I had thought was bleach washed out of my hair. Yes, face down. I'd made the appointment while out with Zamzagul and Nariman on our cell phone quest.

Nur was a well-appointed salon located in the back room on the third floor of a decent-looking department store. Still, in my forty-some years of frequenting beauty parlors, I'd never bent forward over the rinsing bowl. I found it more comfortable than it looked. Surprisingly.

My attempts to describe "foil weave" to the beautician, and to explain I wore my hair "conservative-punk-spiky" were comedic. My fingers wove through the air and I pulled my hair up by its ends. I should have played Charades more often back home.

Nevertheless, the young woman showed me her pile of aluminum foil strips, clearly used, and seemed to know what I wanted. I didn't understand a word, but two hours and 800 *tenge* (about $10) later, I walked out with blonde-highlights framing my face.

No longer "conservative-punk," I now had a cut just like Gulzhahan's. Grateful I was at an age where I no longer fretted over unexpected haircuts, and not yet knowing the blonde highlights I loved would wash out in a few weeks, I was ready for my party.

Back at the apartment, I put on a sleeveless black cotton shift with a strand of raw amber, a necklace that came with a story a few years older than my marriage to Woody. A psychologist from Poland who stuttered had given it to Woody in thanks for Woody's sponsoring him to attend the annual conference of the International Fluency Association, of which Woody was then the president.

"Are you marry-ed?" he had asked Woody, holding the gift in his open hands.

"No, I'm not," Woody had replied.

"Have you luff?" he then asked. With Woody's affirmation that he did indeed have a "love" (me), the man handed the amber necklace to him.

"This is for your luff," he said.

I loved wearing this necklace and, even more, I loved hearing Woody tell the story, complete with the Polish accent he was so good at. But there'd be no droll accented English stories this night, though. Our new friends had a hard enough time following simple English without layering it up with accents.

With my omnipresent Teva sandals on my feet and a beige shawl, this now fifty-six-year-old Grandma was eager to party. Gulzhahan had chosen Robinzone, a restaurant that offered English menus, and we had made reservations for our group of ten for 7 o'clock. When our plans to share a taxi with Symbat and Yergali fell through—at 6:45, Yergali was still not home—Woody asked Symbat to call us a taxi, planning to be there by 7.

Woody's need to be on time in America often bordered on obsession. In Kazakhstan, the attitude toward time couldn't have been more different. "Time, in Kazakhstan," I said in my best sociologist voice, "adjusts to the needs of the people," adding, "We needn't worry."

"Sorry. We said seven, and I want to be there by seven. Earlier is even better."

He really is annoying. But off we went, me not saying anything. Woody told the taxi driver, "Robinzone," in his adopted Russian accent, and, not long after, we got out in a section of town we hadn't yet seen. It was lovely. Shade trees and benches lined wide cement walkways along two sides of a central fountain area, reminiscent of a New England town square. There was grass, too, clumps of it dotted among the trees.

Looking across the street in one direction, I glimpsed the 19th-century American South in a white antebellum-style building that seemed straight out of *Gone With the Wind*. How eagerly I sought the familiar.

On the square, with its back to a fountain, was a large statue of Kuanysh Satpaev, the man who had discovered copper in the nearby village of Satpaev, and invented the method for processing it, obviously a big deal for Zhezkazgan.

Satpaeva *Ulitza* (Street), not surprisingly, ran along one side of the square with a bank building filling up most its length. Filling the entire block across the street on the other side was the imposing banana-yellow building of the Kazakhmys

Corporation, Zhezkazgan's major employer. But nowhere did we see a restaurant.

Our taxi gone, we wandered briefly along the surrounding streets, expecting to find a sign that announced Robinzone. We didn't. With a silent acknowledgment to Woody for our cell phones, I called Zamzagul. It was 7 pm.

Before I finished announcing myself to her, she replied, "I am coming, I am coming," and hung up.

"She hung up," I said to Woody, bemused. He shrugged. I tried Gulzhahan next. "Hi. It's Janet," I began.

Again, as soon as she heard my voice, she cried, "We are coming, we are coming," and hung up.

What a fix. At least we were not keeping them waiting for us at the restaurant. I called Gulzhahan again.

"Don't hang up, don't hang up!" I hollered this time, when she answered.

I could hear her, "We are coming," repeated, but continued with my "don't hang up" mantra in the hope mine would last longer than hers. It certainly was louder.

"We can't find the restaurant," I offered when she finally stopped talking.

"Where are you?"

"At the square," I said, "by the fountain."

"We'll be there. Don't go away." The famous Kazakh hospitality we'd heard so much about was showing itself. Woody and I sat down on a nearby bench to wait. It wasn't long.

Robinzone, it turned out, was tucked behind another restaurant, which looked like a neglected two-story Brooklyn walk-up. Even when we were upon it, we still saw no signage. The inside was dramatically dark after the bright sun we'd been in, but I could see the long, rectangular table set for ten amidst a jungle of plastic plants. We were the first to arrive. The restaurant, at ten past seven, was empty.

I took a seat at the far head of the table, Woody to my right. Gulzhahan and Darkhan sat at the opposite end. Conversation came easily while we waited for the remaining six guests. Gulzhahan was great at translating our words periodically so her husband was part of the conversation.

I liked Darkhan. He was quick to smile a wonderful, dimpled smile that filled his face. Though we couldn't directly exchange more than the Russian equivalent of, "Hello, how are you?" and "Fine, thank you. How are you?" I thought him bright. He was definitely good-looking.

Gulzhahan had told me during training how they met in college where he studied what I deduced was electrical engineering, how Darkhan had proposed to her, and how nervous she'd been when meeting his family for the first time.

I'd learned about their little boy Duman, too. He was then three, and her trip to Almaty had been the first time she'd been away from him.

"I miss my son very much," she'd often said, but never dwelled on it.

Darkhan now worked for "the heating company" in Zhezkazgan, and our conversation moved to the town's centralized single-source heating system.

Through Gulzhahan, Darkhan explained how the Soviet-style system worked. He told us about the pipes we'd seen throughout the town. They formed no particular pattern that we could discern, and ranged in size from as much as four feet in diameter to ones no bigger than an inch. According to Darkhan, all of them carried steam to each building and, eventually, to each apartment, and, I imagined, back to a central furnace miles away.

"One winter," Gulzhahan told us, "a pipe broke. All the people huddled under blankets and tried to stay warm. Some burned trees."

"There are no thermostats in Zhezkazgan apartments," I mused aloud, enjoying the realization that here in this post-Soviet land, even the temperature of one's living quarters was a communal affair.

"No, there are none." And Gulzhahan laughed as she said it.

Talk of freezing winters ended as the other guests arrived and my fifty-sixth birthday party began.

There was one menu for the ten of us. Ordering was also a communal affair. The single menu included many familiar words from our months of training. *Monti* was a dish of large, handmade, meat-filled raviolis, stacked on trays five or six levels high, and steamed. *Pelmini* was a smaller meat-filled ravioli, but either boiled or fried. *Ploff* was similar to our rice pilaf, *galupsi* was stuffed cabbage, and *cutlet* was a Salisbury steak without the gravy. One whole page of the menu was devoted to salads: English, French, American, Olivia. All we had to do was choose. I ordered an Olivia salad, which, disappointingly, had no olives. Woody got the cutlet.

Then we turned to drinks, which was harder. Kazakhs have embraced Russian drinking habits with gusto, and alcohol—mostly vodka, brandy, and wine—is a huge part of every Kazakhstani social gathering. In Kazakhstan, offense is easily taken if you agree to have a drink with one group and then decide not to with another. Here, it would be harder to "just say no" if I'd already just said yes.

I'd decided before we left home not to drink while on our assignment. Since I rarely drank anyway, it was no big deal. Woody is a teetotaler.

Peace Corps would have loved it if all their volunteers were teetotalers. Training sessions *ad nauseum* had drilled home the point that alcohol consumption was a slippery slope. Alcohol, they'd remind us, was too frequently a factor when a volunteer's service ended early.

But that wasn't what made it hard. Woody not only doesn't drink, he doesn't pay for alcohol either, for anyone. That part is a political stance, and I knew he took it seriously. I also knew he'd forgotten to think about the fact that this might come up at my birthday party. What to do?

When the time came to order, I leaned over to him and whispered, "They'll expect alcohol. Do you want to say something?"

He did. He spoke to Zamzagul, seated directly across from him.

"I won't pay for alcohol," he told her curtly. "Will you tell the others?"

No one appeared to mind. "Let's order juice," Zamzagul responded, not skipping a beat. Woody ordered a Pepsi. The others toasted me with juice throughout the meal.

Ah, toasts. There was a full page of Russian toasts in my language workbook, a few of which I'd memorized, but that night I couldn't remember one. It was a moot point, however, for none of the toasts, except for Woody's brief "Z'den rash denya" (Happy Birthday) was in Russian.

Kazakhs take toasts seriously. To them, toasts have power. If enough people wish you "good health," for example, you might just get it. It certainly can't hurt.

Gulzhahan and Zamzagul's husbands went first, during our main course. They spoke in Kazakh and no one translated, but their words were serious, earnest, and sweet. I watched them intently, wishing to make eye contact, but not yet aware that a Muslim man doesn't generally make eye contact with a woman, even one old enough to be his mother. Still, their tone left me feeling genuinely appreciated, accepted. I was glad to be among them.

Zamzagul spoke in English. "Janet, may I give you congratulations on your birthday. I wish for you success in the future, good health, happiness, love. I thank you for being here."

Aniya spoke also during dinner, and Gulzhahan went last, after they'd sung "Happy Birthday" to me and I'd blown out the candles we'd somehow managed to collect.

"Janet, Happy Birthday. I want you to be happy, to teach us many things, and to have good health. I want you to like Zhezkazgan, Kazakhstan, and us."

The toasts touched me, of course. As did the gifts they'd brought: a traditional Kazakh vest, velvet with ornate trim embroidered down the front; a pair of Kazakh bracelets with a stone in each center; a miniature *dombra*, the traditional two-string instrument of Kazakh lore; and a book of Kazakh history, in Kazakh.

But more than their traditional toasts and unexpected gifts, their generosity of spirit, and their evident desire to have good things happen to me surprised me. I'd planned this party to share the way Americans celebrated their birthdays, and ended up learning how warmly Kazakhs embrace one another. I was excited by the prospect that I would share my culture as they shared theirs with me. And I was deeply moved.

I needed to speak. Our training was quite clear that toasts, warm wishes, anything verbal, were always appreciated in the Kazakh culture. And having these friendly people appreciate me was, after all, my goal. I began to tear up as I stood to speak.

"Thank you for sharing my birthday," I began, my voice quivering with emotion. "I'm happy to be here in your very big country."

Everyone was quiet and their eyes followed me.

"I came to do a job, and to do that I have left many things behind." I looked around the table, at each face. *Where to go from here?* "You know I have three young grandchildren."

I paused to picture my two newest grandchildren, cousins born two days apart just months before we left, and to hear again my son David's words whispered in my ear.

"Go now, while they're too young to know you're gone."

Then, I continued. "I have given up watching them grow to come here." Though I was the only grandmother at the table, I counted on the universal value of grandchildren. It was more than time with my grandchildren that I'd given up, though I didn't mention the things I'd left behind. And I certainly didn't mention Merlin, our rescued greyhound.

43

As I stood there, I thought again of the career I'd given up, the home I'd sold, the six-foot long, claw-foot bathtub, the books, the cars. So many things to which I'd been deeply attached. I didn't mention any of them.

Instead I said, "I don't want these next two years to be wasted. I'll need your help to be successful." Then I ended with, "We need to work together. And I will count on you to help me."

How much anyone understood, I'll never know, though I saw Gulzhahan's face nodding throughout. But what I said was important for me to hear; if nothing else, a useful reminder early on that the more I can let go of the old, the more room there is for the new. And it was "the new" for which I yearned, at least in those early weeks.

Chapter Five
A WALK AROUND TOWN

We had to get out of our apartment. It wasn't just the heat or the close quarters where everyone seemed to be tripping over everyone, or the stultifying pall that hung over all who entered. And it wasn't only that Symbat's apartment had grown significantly smaller since her mother had arrived to babysit the night of my birthday party and never left.

Since we were never introduced, I didn't even know her name. There she was night after night, sleeping on the sofa in the living room. Some days, a very quiet boy of about four sat by her as she bustled about the kitchen. We didn't know his name either, or why he was there.

We needed to get out of the apartment because I wanted time with my husband, alone, without the rushing to find cell phones, without the stopping every few minutes to meet a new stranger. Just Woody and me, reconnecting.

And so we left, walking carefully down the dark, urine-infused staircase, past the ghosts of mailboxes past, and out into that spectacularly vibrant sunshine that always reminded me I was happy to be there. For when I was inside, you see, I forgot.

I took Woody's hand as we made our way past the high-tension wires that surely had no place in a residential area, past overflowing garbage bins, and past the still-empty playground.

We walked as fast as Woody could muster. For me, that was slow.

I liked to walk. Always had. One of my fondest memories, now 40 years old, was the hike to the top of New York State's highest peak during my 15th summer. Mount Marcy had beckoned me and I'd spent three days hiking her.

A lot happens in forty years. I'd called seven states and three times that many mailing addresses home. I'd had two children and two degrees, two marriages and two careers. Now, I would spend two years in this new town, this remnant of Soviet omnipresence. That was my commitment: twenty-seven months, actually. Our commitment; I kept forgetting Woody. I squeezed his hand to help me remember.

Woody had been my beacon for nearly ten years. He'd been my first post-awakening relationship, and, when I committed myself to marrying him, I knew it would be a marriage filled with challenge. My inner child, I used to tell him, didn't play well with his. But I said my vows convinced I was partnering with a man as committed to personal growth and introspection as I was.

In his marriage vows, he promised to show me "his strength," something I'd made clear I needed to see more of, his passivity too often a red flag of danger ahead. My vows took a different turn. I promised to never break the spaghetti in half when putting it into the pot, something he'd made clear he wanted.

Genuine, equal partnership was something I'd had no experience with; our vows reflected that. I'd grown up as an only child in a home populated by women. Fresh out of college, I'd married another only child. Late in life, and through a great deal of therapy, I'd learned how to share, how to negotiate. It was a lesson that I wasn't always certain had taken.

Long before my first marriage, my way in the world had consisted of finding a man who knew more than I did and soaking up as much of him as I could. Abandoned at two by my father, and sent off to another state a few months later to live with distant relatives for two years, I'd struggled for over forty years with, as we psychotherapists like to say, "issues of abandonment." At fifty-six, I was still sensitive to being misunderstood, not heard, and not seen.

Woody's "beacon" hadn't been shining on my path of late, and his rock-solid core I'd fallen so in love with had moved upward, into his head, leaving me feeling anxious and unseen. I hoped during this walk to find that tender, strong part of him that I missed. I needed to reassure myself that we were in this adventure together.

Woody, to be fair, had no idea what my agenda was. He just wanted to get outside, away from the odd, unfriendly people we lived with. And, he wanted to spend time with me. He always wanted to spend time with me.

We crossed the street, not in the crosswalk as Woody would have preferred, but in front of the small lean-to where we could wait for the bus under the protective shield from the sun's unremitting glare that he so disdained. For that he would jaywalk.

"I don't think there's a schedule," I told him when he asked when the bus would come. "I think we just wait."

Woody didn't like to wait any more than he liked to walk. He hated to be bored, and waiting put him on the brink of boredom. But, since he had no choice, we waited. Quietly. Still, it was better than waiting in the too-small apartment.

The bus did eventually come, and we climbed on board. I was curious if we'd find anything different on this one than on the buses we'd ridden in Almaty. I found only one. On this particular bus, crowded as they always seemed to be, two teenagers popped up and offered us their seats.

Did we look old? I hoped not. I followed Woody, already in one of the vacated seats.

Sitting next to him, I relaxed into the moment, remembering how well we always seemed to fit together, no matter what the situation. In the two years preceding our departure for the Peace

Corps, we'd been focused myopically on getting ourselves through the medical clearance phase of our application. Tests, procedures, physical therapy, dental caps, all had been accomplished as required. Here we were.

I reached over and took his hand again, settling our entwined fingers on my lap and remembering all the places we'd been in the ten years we'd known each other. We'd seen Scandinavia, England, Europe, and Australia giving workshops for people who stuttered and the professionals who treated them. And we saw Mexico, Costa Rica, Jamaica, and Key West on our own, just for adventure's sake.

Shortly before we'd finally married, I'd quit my last fundraising job in the increasingly bureaucratic, corporate world that the university had become, finished the training I'd begun three years earlier, and hung my shingle as a Certified Gestalt Psychotherapist. The first few years of our marriage had been good ones. I expected the rest to be just as good. Yes, expected.

We got off the bus and wandered the dusty sidewalks. I was eager for us to see the town together, share our impressions, and compare notes. I was not eager, however, to hear Woody's conversation filled with complaining. He didn't like the heat. There was too much dust. The buildings were ugly.

Our first stop would be at the post office to see if we could get the PO Box we knew we needed. But we got there only to find they were closed. We'd forgotten that everything except restaurants closed for lunch, though not all at the same time. We sat on the low concrete wall that ran the length of the post office block as I fumbled in my rucksack for the book of maps to see where to go next.

The thin book was full of useful information for the newly transplanted, even though it was in Kazakh and used the Cyrillic alphabet. I could sound the words out and Woody could translate enough of them into English. The entire town was divided onto separate pages; every street represented, each building outlined. ATMs, bus stops, the public *banya* (bath house), pharmacies, even the town's museum were identified with easy-to-understand symbols. We located the restaurant, Aiya, where we'd eaten with Zamzagul and Nariman, four blocks away.

"Let's have lunch," we both proclaimed at once, and looked up just as an old woman with a scarf on her head—a quintessential *babushka* (grandmother)—came up the few steps from the sidewalk and began running toward us, yelling and waving an arm. We stood up to meet her as she approached, but she stopped immediately when we stood. Then, she turned and went on her way into the post office.

"You think that was what we heard about?" I asked Woody.

He nodded, "Must have been."

During training, we'd heard stories of volunteers being pulled physically off concrete steps or sometimes up off a stone floor by half-crazed *babushka*s. We'd heard about the prohibition, the superstition, against sitting on concrete. It was either sterility that was at risk, or back pain; we'd heard both.

We just shrugged and walked toward the restaurant. Woody, much to my disappointment, stayed a step or two ahead of me where I couldn't reach for his hand.

I thought Zhezkazgan was a nice town, despite its gulag history and the heavy metals in its water. Forgetting the screaming *babushka* at the post office, there was a good energy to it. People filled the walkways, all seeming to be going somewhere, busy with their lives.

A block away we found a stunning exception to the general beige hue of the land: a bed of bright red tulips in front of a building called Saryarka. I was glad to see the colorful and obviously well-watered flowers, particularly when I discovered (thanks to my book of maps) that Saryarka was not only a nightclub and a bowling alley, it was also the town's movie theater.

I needed a movie theater for the community project I was planning. Every Peace Corps volunteer is supposed to organize a community project of some kind, in addition to our assigned work duties. I'd decided during training that mine would be weekly English language movies from America.

"Look, Woody," I said, eagerly. "If the owner of this theater can afford to plant and water tulips in the middle of this arid steppe, surely he can afford to give my students a discount once a week."

I felt giddy as pieces of my new life began to fall into place. Woody nodded, acknowledging that he'd heard me, but he didn't stop.

He's so eager to get to the restaurant and order lunch, I complained silently. *What happened to our walk together to help us reconnect?*

My sense of separateness from Woody dissipated as I went back to thinking of my community project. *I'll have to find donors for the movies; I'll need to advertise; I'll need to create vocabulary lists for difficult words.* I had until February to begin the project, and this was late August. There was plenty of time. Still, I loved planning.

Four more blocks flew by before we reached the tiny restaurant and settled into an empty table against the far wall. Inside, the restaurant was refreshingly cool, though filled with annoying cigarette smoke. When the *shashlik* we'd ordered arrived, we found it looked just like *shish kabob* without the vegetables: marinated cubes of lamb, skewered and grilled over an open fire. *Shashlik* is served with fresh bread, a dish of chopped raw onion, and vinegar in a sprinkle bottle.

We ate quickly, downed our Coca-Colas, paid our 350-*tenge* tab (about $3), and started out the door.

"Let's hold off on the post office. It'll be open all afternoon," I said to Woody. "I'd like to walk down that street with the park in the middle of it. Let's see where that goes."

I was in no hurry to get back to Symbat's apartment. And, still hoping to feel connected again to Woody, I wanted to draw this outdoor exploration out as long as I could.

"Sure," he replied, with a sigh of resignation. I knew Woody hated to walk; I just didn't know what else to do.

We turned down Seifullina, a street with a wide median filled with the short, squat trees that were everywhere.

Many of the streets throughout the country had been renamed when the Communists lost power. This one, previously named Boulvar Kosmonavtov—Boulevard of the Cosmonauts—was now named after a Kazakh hero, Saken Seifullin, a young academic who had been executed during the Stalin era. But, though the streets now bore Kazakh names, they did so using Russian language rules.

We crossed the double lanes of traffic at a light and turned down the median strip. I was eager to grab Woody's hand once again and stroll through this as-close-to-a-park-as-we-could-find area. But the ground beneath our feet had dry irrigation ditches among the trees and we needed to pay attention.

We walked single file so we wouldn't trip, and quickly abandoned our meandering, crossing the second set of double lanes to the far sidewalk. There, I decidedly grabbed Woody's hand, intertwined our fingers, and hung on tight.

Near the end of the street, beyond a rusted and evidently forgotten memorial to the "conquerors of outer space," I saw water: a lake, perhaps, or maybe a reservoir or river. I took a deep breath in excitement as I noticed the small beach and people swimming and, as I pulled out my camera, Woody turned to walk back to the post office.

"Wait," I called. "I want to take some pictures."

"Of what? It's pretty bleak."

"It's different. The water looks refreshing. Maybe we can swim sometime."

"Probably not. I'm sure it's polluted."

I sighed. His negativity was growing. His unexpected tentativeness, hesitancy to embrace new ways, and resistance to see past his own ethnocentrism had made him a stranger to me. I focused only on the fact that in the ten years I'd known him, negativity had never been one of his traits. Just the opposite; I'd once called him a Pollyanna, in fact, in reference to his insatiable ability to burrow deep into the denial that was taught him as a boy growing up in the Christian Science religion.

"They raised denial to a fine art form," he'd once told me, trying his best to explain the odd collection of beliefs that his mother had lived by.

His overt negativity scared me. I was afraid it would spiral into a realization that our coming had been a mistake. We'd given up too much to be here. I had, anyway; the things Woody had given up—his boat, his car, and his bread-making machine—could be replaced. I felt no sympathy for him. *I've given up too much*, I angrily recalled.

Defiantly, I snapped a few photos, then hurried to catch up with him. Thus began a practice that had been all too familiar in marriage #1: I'd feel disconnected and ignore it. My husband would fall quietly into his own world and I'd feel even farther away. I'd never expected to fall back into that pattern with Woody.

On our way back to the post office, I grabbed his hand one last time, only to realize just how frustrated I was with him.

This outing had left me more unsettled than before. I'd expected fresh air and some adventurous exploration would realign our internal gyroscopes. Instead, just the opposite had happened. I'd become more aware of just how irritated and angry I was at nearly everything he said or did—sure signs of culture shock for both of us, but I didn't think of it at the time. I just wanted him to change back.

Culture shock is disorienting at best. Our grand adventure was to be filled with strange new ways, things we wouldn't understand, questions that seemed to have no answers. And for the first three months, during our training, that's just what we found.

In Almaty, our outings and field trips with our cohorts, and our life with our host family—every strange new experience— was exciting, and we embraced the many differences with glee, classically infatuated with this exotic new land.

Now that honeymoon phase was over. And, it appeared to be over in my marriage as well.

Chapter Six
SCHOOL

School, and therefore the work we'd come to do, was scheduled to start ten days after we arrived. It was none-too-soon for either of us. And the day after our wander around the town alone, Woody and I had a chance to tour our respective institutions and meet our respective bosses.

Woody's supervisor at his university was Zamzagul who had taken us around town with her husband in our aborted quest for cell phones. She ran the English department of the improbably but officially named "Zhezkazgan University Named After O. A. Baikonurov," an academician and scientist of the 19th century who specialized in mining engineering. Woody called it simply "The U."

Back on the day I'd bought my cell phone with Gulzhahan, Woody had gone with Zamzagul to meet her boss, the university rector. Walking over with Zamzagul, he'd explained (apologetically) to her that his PhD was not in English, but in Speech Pathology.

"But," he told me later that night, "she just said, 'That's okay. You are native speaker.'" His dismay was tangible. "No department chair in an American university would hire someone to teach a subject that was different from the one their degree was in. I don't think she even knows what Speech Pathology is."

We knew from the Peace Corps staff that it was quite unusual for a volunteer to come in with a PhD, so Woody expected his advanced degree, plus his thirty-five years of experience, would be of particular value to whatever university got him. Zamzagul's reaction may have left him dismayed. But his conversation with the rector was downright disappointing.

"He didn't seem to know or care much about my qualifications," Woody told me. "I'm just a volunteer."

For someone who'd expected to be well utilized during his two years, Woody was dumbstruck. No one seemed the least impressed by either his advanced degree or level of experience, even his colleagues. I had no idea he'd gone into the Peace Corps with such expectations.

"They were cordial and welcoming," he reported. "But any particular deference I'll get isn't because of my teaching experience and education. It's because I'm old."

Still, he looked forward to being the resident "expert" on all things American: a surefire set up, I thought smugly, for disappointment.

My situation was different. I felt I didn't have any "qualifications" other than being a native speaker, and I was fine with that.

I'd worked hard to leave behind any expectations, once I'd identified them. But they had a way of sneaking in anyway. Like they did when I met the director of my college.

When Gulzhahan, who was technically my supervisor, said it was time for me to meet the man who sat at the top of Zhezkazgan Humanitarian College, where I would be working for the next two years, I expected an informal chat. Of course, I didn't recognize that as an expectation until that informal chat turned into something else.

At the appointed time, Gulzhahan greeted me at the college's main entrance with a hug and ushered me into the director's office and onto a chair by the far wall. Half a dozen important-looking women were seated on chairs on two sides of the room. A few of them had a wide grin for me as I settled into my seat, while the others, involved in conversation, gave me cursory glances. I didn't know who they were; introductions were painfully absent.

In Kazakhstan, if we even got an introduction, we rarely got a name. Instead, we got a role. I'd met mothers and fathers, brothers and sisters, aunts and uncles, and friends and colleagues throughout my training. All had remained nameless. Somehow, it had felt rude and intrusive to ask for someone's name. Early on, during our training weeks, I'd stopped asking.

So here I was, seated among a small group of friendly enough faces, but with no idea who they were or why these particular people had come to meet me. Except, of course, for the director.

I was glad I'd worn my "modest yet American" outfit: denim skirt—the longest I owned—a green long-sleeved top with a high scooped neck, and Teva sandals. When I offered my version of the Kazakh hello, a mutilated version of "*salye metsiz be*" (I found *Sally misses beer* easier to remember), they laughed, good-naturedly. I hoped they were impressed by my attempt, but more likely they were amused by my poor pronunciation.

The director, a pudgy man with a ruddy complexion topped by thinning hair, sat at an oversized desk to my right, just beyond where Gulzhahan stood. Seated behind his massive desk, he appeared even smaller than he was. He wore a white shirt open at the collar, as though he'd tired of his tie. I heard my name a few times, as he talked directly to Gulzhahan and offered me an odd smile now and again. Murmurs wafted around the room and the unknown women smiled at me while I sat, hands folded in my lap, listening to the dialogue between my counterpart and the director.

I thought Gulzhahan seemed uncomfortable in her role, which in my brief experience with her was unusual. But when I tried to pinpoint just what she was doing that gave me this impression, I realized it wasn't what she was doing differently, it was what she wasn't doing. She wasn't laughing.

In the few weeks I'd known Gulzhahan, I couldn't remember a time when her speech wasn't punctuated with laughter. Good laughter, the kind that's contagious, heartfelt. No. Here in the director's office, there was no laughter, and this surprised me.

Listening to her talking to the director, my sense was that something was off. Did this little man hold some special power over her? Finally, the director glanced at me, smiled and nodded intimately, as if we shared some inside joke. I had only his body language to go on, but he seemed to want to take me out for a drink. He gave me the chills.

I expected a few questions or comments from the women sitting passively on two sides of the room. But their purpose appeared to be more formality than function.

Abruptly, Gulzhahan turned to me.

"Would you like to say something?"

I was startled. "Should I say something?" I asked, counting on the fact that we were the only two who understood English. I certainly had nothing prepared.

"Yes. It would be nice."

A little advance notice would have been nice!

Thanks to my stuttering history, giving impromptu speeches had once thrown me into paralysis. And while those stuttering days were long gone, the old wiring, the programming of those early years, was still there. I consciously reminded myself that even if I stuttered, even if the worst possible thing might happen, whatever that might be, I would still be okay. This little internal dialogue had helped me through myriad public speaking moments in the 20 years since I'd first emerged from my metaphorical closet. And, once again, it worked.

All eyes were expectantly on me and I fell into a shortened version of my birthday toast.

"I am very happy to be here," I said, in English, "and I am looking forward to doing a good job, with Gulzhahan's help and your help."

Gulzhahan translated and the women smiled and nodded.

Compared to the creepy director, these women looked friendly, gracious, and kind. I was curious about them. We'd be working in the same building for the next two years and I wondered just how well I'd get to know them over those years. I hoped I'd at least learn their names.

I followed Gulzhahan out of the room, the Napoleonic director still behind his desk, and let out a long sigh. I hadn't realized I'd been holding my breath; I wasn't used to being leered at.

"What can you say about the director?" I asked Gulzhahan, thinking it only fair to know her take before I gave her mine.

She just shrugged, unwilling to say anything about him. I gave an exaggerated shudder and she smiled a knowing smile at me. I knew we had the same feeling about him. We didn't need words.

Quickly flipping into tour-guide mode, Gulzhahan showed me around the rest of the building, including the teacher's lounge, a long narrow room five flights up that was packed full of dilapidated furniture, but still felt empty.

How different it will be when filled with people, I thought—another expectation bubbling up.

In less than a week, I would find out. And I couldn't wait!

September 1, my first day of work, rolled around at last. Forty years after first thinking about Peace Corps, two years in the application process, ten weeks of training, and ten days in Zhezkazgan getting settled, I was finally off to my first day of work as a Peace Corps volunteer.

Throughout the country, all schools began on September 1, Knowledge Day. I was as eager as I'd ever been to start school, with sharpened pencils in my rucksack, the small notebook and pen I always carried, my digital camera, and a heart bursting with excitement.

Woody had left for his Knowledge Day celebration earlier, needing a bus to take him across town. But Zhezkazgan Humanitarian College was just a ten-minute walk from Symbat's apartment. I walked eagerly past rows of painted cement-block apartments on one side and single-family homes hidden behind neglected metal fencing on the other, until I saw the school building: a five-story concrete structure that towered above everything around it.

As I reached the college courtyard, I could see it was full of students talking and laughing in small groups. The few young men standing in their own clusters were dressed in traditional western suit coats and ties. Though the crowd was mostly female, this could have been the first day of school almost anywhere in the United States. Western dress prevailed, though the skirts were shorter, the tops tighter, and the heels higher than I'd expect to see in an academic setting.

I walked among the students looking for Gulzhahan, saying an occasional "*dobra utra*" (the Russian good morning), or the more formal "*drast v'witchya*" (the Russian hello) to anyone who caught my eye. Though I found it odd that few responded, my excitement mounted.

How many of these young people will be my students? What will I be teaching them?

I moved through two sets of double doors and climbed the short dark staircase. On the first floor, down a short hallway to my left, were a few offices. I looked into the director's office and called out my Kazakh *Sally misses beer* to him as he sat at his desk. He smiled and gave me a thumbs-up. *I should probably learn his name*, I thought, but the idea of even that much familiarity made my skin crawl.

I had greeted him in Kazakh, knowing he was Kazakh. Yet, I'd greeted the students outside in Russian. I stood a moment, confused, when a female student approached me.

"Come with me," she said, and steered me into an office across from the director's.

No doubt she was told to go get the American, I thought.

We walked in on a tall, dark-haired woman in a white business suit who stood at her desk checking her makeup in a compact mirror. She gave me a warm, welcoming smile and shook my hand with a strong grip. I recognized her from my "debut" a few days before, though I still didn't know her name or what she did there. She was a handsome middle-aged woman who reminded me of my own mother when I was growing up. She spoke to the student, and then nodded in my direction.

"She wants to spend time with you to practice her English," the student who brought me translated.

I envisioned long lunches, meanderings through town together, with me speaking English and she absorbing all I taught. I was game.

"Fine with me," I said, "That's why I'm here." I smiled back at the woman and took my rucksack off to fit into a nearby chair.

The fact was, female friendships were a vital part of my mental health, and I fervently hoped to form new ones in Kazakhstan. I cherished the conversations Woody and I had—or used to have, anyway—but I wanted the laughter that comes when women get together. He and I were so serious when we talked. And, while I would stay in touch with friends in Ohio, Pennsylvania, and Virginia during those two years, whether through email or via the care packages they sent, I wanted flesh-and-blood friends in the here and now, female friends. This woman had definite friend potential.

As I settled into the chair and the student began translating a conversation between my potential new friend and me, Gulzhahan appeared, and any plans I might have made evaporated. Gulzhahan nodded at the woman and shuffled me away.

"What does she do here?" I asked as Gulzhahan and I paused for me to catch my breath on our way up the stairwell to the teachers' lounge. Five flights of stairs was something I would have to get used to. "And what is her name?"

"Bakhit. She is the director's assistant," Gulzhahan reported. "She is in charge of the courses the students take." Effectively this made her Gulzhahan's boss.

Still, she looked about my age. And she was so friendly. But, thoughts of my future friendship dissolved as Gulzhahan and I walked through the shell of what was once a language lab and into the teachers' lounge, now filled with two groups of young women laughing and talking among themselves: the English teachers.

Only two weeks earlier, while on the train ride to Zhezkazgan, I'd asked Gulzhahan to give me the names of my future colleagues so I could memorize them before school started. The oddness of the local names, I'd found during our weeks of training, had made it particularly difficult for me to remember them, and I wanted all the help I could get.

On that particular Saturday morning, as our train had bounced its way across the Kazakh steppe, I'd written down their first names in Cyrillic letters, then in Latin letters, and finally in a phonetic transliteration. When my lists were complete, they'd shown only sixteen names.

"You said there were seventeen teachers," I'd reminded Gulzhahan.

"Janet. You forgot Janet," she'd said with her wide, contagious smile, and I'd added my name to the list, *Dzhanet*.

I looked around now, eager to put those names to faces. Including Gulzhahan and me, I counted nine female teachers. Three were involved with a curling iron in front of the mirror and four were gathered around a small bathroom scale, giggling.

"These are our teachers," Gulzhahan said to me with a wave of her hand, the extent of her introductions.

"Good morning. Hello," I said, assuming they'd understand. They were English teachers, after all. I also secretly hoped they'd prefer to practice their English with me rather than have me speak Russian with them.

Russian. I still hadn't caught on to the fact that the official state language of the country was no longer Russian, but Kazakh. Zhezkazgan Humanitarian College was a Kazakh language institution, not a Russian one.

My co-workers were Kazakh, not Russian. Of course they'd be speaking Kazakh. But even more pertinent, why would anyone care to speak Russian, the language of their former oppressors, if they didn't have to? But the Peace Corps had trained me in Russian, or tried to, so Russian was the foreign language that came first to my tongue.

Fortunately, English was what they spoke to me.

"Here, you get on," one of the young women said to me as though she'd known me for years, and she stepped off the scale to make way.

I nodded at everyone and smiled shyly. Here was a cultural difference I could see clearly and I embraced it immediately, equally curious about my weight and eager to do away with formality. I hopped on.

According to the scale and our conversion calculations from kilos to pounds, either of which could well have been off, I'd lost twelve pounds since I'd been weighed during training. I was thrilled to see each of the pounds gone.

Music from the Knowledge Day ceremony in the courtyard below broke our gigglefest at the scale, and I followed the others as they hurried downstairs to the courtyard. People congregated in thick groups, perhaps ten people deep, leaving a center area open.

Along one side, in the shade of a stand of thick brush and a few trees, two young men sang what sounded like a lively, popular song. They were good, particularly the taller one. They each had a microphone attached to an amplification system—a more sophisticated system than I would expect, given the sparsely furnished classrooms I had seen. I assumed the song was in Kazakh, though it could have been in Russian. Heck, it could've been in Portuguese and I wouldn't have known the difference then.

All those critical Russian sentences I'd memorized in order to squeak through my Peace Corps language test were rapidly disappearing because I never used them. In fact, the only Russian I heard in those early weeks was Woody's occasional attempts to speak Russian to our oh-so-resistant host parents. Since our arrival nearly two weeks before, I'd spoken only English.

Outside in the courtyard, I was reminded that not all the teachers in this college spoke English. I still hadn't grasped that the reason nothing sounded remotely familiar was that they weren't speaking Russian; they were speaking Kazakh. *Would I ever be able to talk to them?*

Following more songs and more than a few speeches, a few teachers and students received awards for accomplishments I couldn't discern. Gulzhahan translated for me now and again. I understood little, but enjoyed the fast-paced and happy atmosphere. It was a true celebration. And all on a spectacularly sunny day, under a sky of bright, vibrant blue. I couldn't get enough of that sky.

Just as the awards were winding down and I thought we might finally get to work, someone suddenly pushed me forward and I heard my name over the speakers. I was being introduced as one of three new teachers at the school that year. How nice. I smiled. The crowd applauded. Then the English teachers (including me) went out for lunch. There would be no work that first day.

Apparently, Knowledge Day, a gift of the Soviets, offers first graders a chance to see their school building, meet their teachers, and think positively about school. Just like the seven-year-olds, I also saw my building, met my fellow teachers, and came away with a positive attitude toward school. I was in. And it felt good. Work would wait.

While I would teach English to future primary school English teachers, Woody would be teaching English to students who aspired to become interpreters and translators of English. His students were a few years older than mine. Some were graduates of my college, while others had come directly from high school.

He had been so looking forward to stepping into the role of resident "expert" on all things American, yet he would never feel connected to his colleagues.

There was a handful of explanations as to why Woody would be excluded from the inner sanctum of his department, forever the outsider. For one, he was the only English-speaking male in the department, and socializing between the genders did not come as easily as it might in the States. For another, he was the only teetotaler in a department whose "tea parties" would consistently include vodka, wine, and brandy.

Those reasons were enough, but Woody also lacked, from my perspective, an inherent curiosity about the Kazakh culture. And I found myself feeling repeatedly disappointed by this, as I was when he reported on his Knowledge Day ceremony.

Like mine, his had also been in an outdoor courtyard, complete with music and speeches.

"They played their national anthem, but no one seemed to know it," he told me. "But the oddest thing happened."

"Oh?"

I'd just finished giving him the run-down of my first day and was eager to hear his. But if mine had included their national anthem, I certainly had no idea.

"Zamzagul asked me what we do when our national anthem is played."

"What did you tell her?"

"I told her, 'We put our hands over our hearts and sing,'" he said, pausing for effect, as though thinking, *what else could I say?*

"But then she turned and yelled at the teachers and students. Something like, 'In America, everyone sings their national anthem.'"

Woody shook his head as he told me, amazed that Zamzagul would shame her students so overtly, so publicly.

Once again, I felt that stab of disappointment that I was getting each time Woody and I disagreed. This time, my sympathies were with Zamzagul. Yelling at students was a common "teaching" tool in the former Soviet system. If he judged Zamzagul for yelling, then I judged him for judging. That last part skipped my notice entirely, of course.

"How did you first learn the *Star Spangled Banner?*" I asked, remembering grade school music classes and lessons on Francis Scott Key hiding in Baltimore Harbor.

"I'm not sure. Probably baseball games," he answered.

Americans know their national anthem, even if we might not sing it easily. We've grown up with it. Kazakhs haven't. They've had neither baseball games nor class lectures about their anthem's history. Indeed, they didn't even teach Kazakh history in the schools until after 1991.

But an even bigger difference between our two stories was the melody. While our *Star Spangled Banner*'s melody once sang the praises of wine and ale, the melody of Kazakhstan's anthem at the time was from an old Soviet folk song. It wasn't fair to fault the Kazakhs for not singing with gusto, just as it wasn't fair to fault Zamzagul for using one of the primary tools she'd been taught: yelling.

But Woody wasn't the least bit curious about any of this, and my disappointment in him grew. I wanted him back the way I remembered him. I missed him terribly.

I climbed into bed that night feeling miserable. I was sick: this was my fourth day struggling with what I'd dubbed Genghis Khan's revenge. I was disoriented by my inability to absorb the language. And I was out of sync with the one person I'd consistently been on the same page with for the past ten years.

Falling asleep was difficult. Lying awake, staring at the ceiling, I thought of my two new grandbabies, now nearly a year old. Were they standing yet? I'd gotten used to having the Internet available to me during training, but we'd been cut off from home since we'd arrived because of Internet issues, and that mounting sense of separation was starting to take a toll. I'd sent letters, certainly. But we didn't even have a post office box yet to receive letters, and the separation weighed on me like a boulder on my chest.

As the sleepless hours continued, I thought, too, of the clients I'd had at the end of my practice. I wondered how they were faring. At least my sons would keep me posted on the progress of the grandkids, eventually. These clients, I knew, I'd never hear of again.

Yes, I was homesick.

Chapter Seven
SURPRISES IN STORE

Zhezkazgan, a town with fewer than 100,000 people, had thirteen secondary schools, five colleges, and one university. Each secondary school included a primary school (first through fifth grades) a basic school (sixth through eighth grades) and a high school (ninth to eleventh grades). There was no kindergarten as we know it in the United States, nor was there a twelfth grade.

Among the thirteen secondary schools was the Turkish *Lyceum*, where parents who wanted their sons to have an exemplary education in Math, Science, Turkish, and English paid 3,000 *tenge* a month—about $22, but still a lot of money for them—for the opportunity; and a *Gymnasium*, School #8, which also offered a more rigorous academic education, but offered it coeducationally and free.

In between the secondary schools and the single university—where Woody taught—were five colleges, two of them part of Woody's University: an English language college that taught future interpreters and translators and a mining engineer's college.

Independent of Zhezkazgan University, the three other colleges were a medical college, a law college, and a pedagogical college, where I taught. My students would graduate with a diploma to teach English in the primary grades.

I didn't understand this overarching structure of local education at first. I also didn't understand the simple fact that my college worked in two shifts. From eight o'clock in the morning to one o'clock in the afternoon, seventeen English teachers plus about twenty teachers of other subjects taught future primary school English teachers. Then, from one o'clock until six pm, a new set of teachers came in to teach a new set of students to be (non-English-speaking) primary school teachers and *kindergarten* nurses.

Kindergarten. Even that was not what I thought it was. Kazakh *kindergarten* is what we would call pre-school or day care. In any case, I struggled to fit the round peg of half-day classes into the square hole of college life as I had always known it. Once Woody labeled it "shift work," it made better sense.

Zhezkazgan Humanitarian College was a Kazakh-language college in a country where most people had grown up speaking Russian. Since most classes—Pedagogy, Psychology, Anatomy and Children's Physiology, Biology, Chemistry, World History, and many others—were taught in Kazakh, special Russian language groups were created for those students who didn't speak Kazakh. They had their own Russian-speaking teacher, Rustam. This was also hard for me to wrap my mind around.

What I did know was that by the third day of school, I still didn't know what I'd be teaching or when, in which room, or even how many students I'd have. And my equanimity in the midst of this seeming chaos was due, simply, to our training. What a difference a little advance notice can make!

"You won't see a schedule until weeks into the semester," a volunteer from the Peace Corps group ahead of us had said during one of our training weeks.

That simple forewarning, knowing it wasn't just my college that didn't have its act together, made a difference.

Why couldn't they put the schedule together over the summer? It wasn't criticism that led to this question; it was more my inner sociologist's curiosity. Form follows function—the 19th-century mantra from biology that had made the rounds into other disciplines throughout the 20th century—settled in my head and wouldn't leave.

Here was the form, an annually occurring event (the absence of an expected schedule) that persisted year after year and—if the many Peace Corps volunteers who had reported it were taken as a representative sample—in all regions of this large country. What function did this apparent dysfunction serve? That was my question.

So, as the first week ended, I set about developing a working hypothesis. I found it at Rosa's desk when Gulzhahan and I went in to add me to the schedule one very early morning the second week of school.

Like Bakhit, Rosa was one of four assistant directors, and her office was on the first floor, but on the other side of the stairwell from the director's. It had the trappings of a typical office: long bookshelf along one wall and desk floating out from the wall, positioned so Rosa could keep an eye on the door just behind whomever sat across from her. A ceiling-high window behind her let the sunshine fall over her shoulders.

Gulzhahan and I entered the room and squeezed off to the side while other teachers ahead of us had their turn. Rosa was sitting at her desk with a pencil in hand, a gigantic master schedule across the top. I watched her erasing and writing on the schedule as a heavyset, buxom teacher spoke rapidly and pointed to the spot she wanted.

There was negotiating, though I had no idea what the words were. Negotiating in any language has a predictable back-and-forth rhythm that was all too apparent. And there was lots of erasing.

A second teacher, fashionably dressed in a beige suit, complained about what the first had just gotten, which was followed by more erasing.

If I had to write the caption for this picture, it would be, "teachers streamed in and out of her office declaring the absolute necessity for their class to meet at whatever time they had determined rather than the time they were currently assigned."

Rosa methodically erased the class that held the needed time slot and penciled in the new one. And she'd do it again and again. She did it for us, too. I was fascinated.

"We don't know how many students will be here until classes begin," Gulzhahan told me in response to my asking why Rosa couldn't put the schedule together over the summer. "So we don't know how many groups there will be."

"Why can't they give a deadline for students to register, say August 14? Then Rosa would have two weeks to get the schedule set."

But Gulzhahan just smiled at me. "This is how we do it," she said and laughed. My working hypothesis, then, was that schedulers in schools across the country—Rosa, in our case—had to juggle not only the various student groups, they had to accommodate the teachers, particularly those who had seniority. Then there were the rooms and the times to factor in.

A computer program could make short shrift of it all, I reasoned, and thought of my friend Vivian in Virginia whose son could surely write such a program on his lunch break. But I went no further. For all I knew there were other needs being met by what only looked to me like chaos. I wasn't about to change a countrywide system. At least that much of it I understood.

As Gulzhahan and I walked down the hall toward the stairs to go back up to the teacher's lounge, I could see classes were being taught in the classrooms we passed. I seemed to be the only one not yet teaching.

"How do the students know which rooms to use?" I asked.

"They check the board."

Gulzhahan led me past the stairwell and down the hall. There, on the wall opposite Bakhit's office, was a paper much like the one I'd seen on Rosa's desk. It was handwritten in

72

Kazakh, which meant the Cyrillic alphabet, and in cursive. There was no way I'd be reading it.

"The students look here. Teachers, too," she said as she showed me the different columns and rows. Eventually, she told me, the requests would stop and the official schedule would be posted outside Bakhit's office, in ink. Then Rosa's diva days would be over.

Gulzhahan and I turned back to the stairs and climbed the five flights to the teachers' lounge. I still didn't know what I'd teach or to whom. And I certainly didn't know where or when.

I found an empty chair and tried to stay out of the way of the sixteen teachers bustling about the lounge. I couldn't match the names I'd memorized with the faces, but I enjoyed watching them, saying the occasional hello or good-morning as they nodded to me.

Gulzhahan sat at the single desk in the corner by the window. She was in director-mode now and spoke definitively, sharply, but with laughter, too, to each young teacher who stopped at her perch to consult her. No one argued with her, though some looked disappointed as they walked away. I wasn't sure about what.

After about thirty minutes of this, Gulzhahan called me over and introduced me to Raisa. One of the teachers I'd been watching, she was a short, young woman, like Gulzhahan, but with wavy dark longish hair. Raisa gave me a friendly smile, exposing beautiful, straight, white teeth, something I didn't often see in Kazakhstan.

"Raisa is teaching Practical Speaking today." Gulzhahan said. "You will sit in. See how our classrooms are."

Good. I was ready for something to do. And definitely curious.

73

Raisa's outfit, a light-colored suit with stockings and heels, was more professional than my open-toed sandals, no stockings, and denim skirt. But no one seemed to care and I was comfortable. She spoke softly and exuded a sense of tranquility that I found contagious in the midst of such chaos. I was eager to see her in front of a class and I followed her out of the room and down the hall like a puppy.

Together, we walked into Room 42 and the entire class of thirteen students stood as one, chairs scraping the floor in unison as they chorused an English, "Good morning, teachers."

I smiled and gave out a cheery, "Good morning," in English, while Raisa responded with a much more serious but soft, "Good morning, students. Please sit down."

I'd heard about this formality during training, but the actual experience of it felt odd, punitive in some way. Raisa's gentleness was still there, and she gave the students a great smile, but she had turned into "headmistress-marm."

The students, all girls, filled most of the seats in the tiny classroom. I found an empty one in the back row while Raisa called attendance. As she went down her list of thirteen names, I looked around.

It was a small room, just big enough for two rows of five or six double desks and the teacher's desk in the front. The chairs, the desks, even the molding on the white walls, were painted a slightly paler version of the blue of the Kazakhstani flag.

Along the outside wall, just above the solid line of radiators, ceiling-high windows brought in the sunlight but held no curtains to soften their lines. Behind me, along the narrow back wall, ornately framed photographs of ancient men, some in Kazakh garb, some in Western, stared anonymously down at me.

Behind Raisa, a blackboard filled the front wall. All seemed typical until I stared at the fourth wall, the one where alphabet posters might hang, or maps, or verb conjugation diagrams. That wall was bare.

How much work it must take to learn here, I thought, as I sat in my hard, wooden chair in the back of the somewhat barren room.

My own college days and my graduate years had been spent in buildings with central air conditioning, in rooms decorated in colors favored by the architects and designers hired to choose them. They held audiovisual equipment, libraries, charts, and various other accoutrements, depending upon the level and the times.

These students, though, would sit in this room where the blackboard needed to be recoated. Their various teachers would come and go, teaching their assigned subject and carrying with them whatever aids they might need, leaving the students to stay behind under the somber gaze of the framed old men.

Raisa read from an English grammar textbook. She read slowly and repeated often, enabling the students, heads bent over blue copybooks, to get every word. In her gentle voice, she read about verbs: transitive, intransitive, regular, irregular, and modal verbs. She named twelve tenses and read the rules for uses of each. And all the while, the students wrote. It had been forty years since my last grammar class and I'd forgotten English verbs were so complex.

Though a fine lesson on verbs, this was a "Practical Speaking" class, which I interpreted as Practice Speaking, and I was suddenly aware that no one was speaking.

I was more resolved than ever to make a difference. What that difference might be, I still had no idea. Fun came to mind; perhaps I could make learning fun. If only I could talk to these young women, we'd find a way to connect.

"Janet, will you come to the front?" Raisa asked near the end of the class time, jolting me out of my reflections at the back of the room.

As I walked down the center aisle, I wondered what she'd have me do. I hadn't prepared anything.

I had been saying that a lot lately.

"How shall we call you?" Raisa asked me when I reached the front of the room. The students called her Raisa Kussainova, her first name plus her patronymic, the standard professional moniker. If I'd thought about patronymics, I might have suggested Janet Walterovna, from my father's first name plus the appropriate ending. But I assumed my choice was between Janet and Ms. Givens.

"Janet is fine," I offered. These were, after all, college students, young adults. I'd use their first names and they'd use mine—that old American fairness virtue.

"My students would like to ask you questions."

Wonderful, I thought, curious what the questions might be. I was finally going to stand in front of some actual students and was eager to tackle any question they posed. Bring 'em on, I thought, excitedly. Still, I never expected what I got.

"Do you like Michael Jackson?" Huh? Michael Jackson? My mind raced through the little I knew about Michael Jackson: The Jackson Five. Boy wonder. He lived in some fairyland-like fortress; children abounding, something creepy there, but not sure what. I could talk about his album *Thriller* that I'd once won in some contest; that would do.

"I liked *Thriller*," I cautiously offered. That encouraged them.

"Do you know Michael Jackson?" someone asked from the back.

"No. I don't know Michael Jackson," I told her, equally surprised at her naiveté and my own irritation. Did she not realize how big America is? "I've never met him."

"Did you see *Titanic*?" a young girl in front asked.

Ah! A question I could answer easily.

"Yes. I did," I told her. "And I liked it very much."

"I love Leonardo DiCaprio," she added, pronouncing his name without a trace of accent and with much teenage infatuation.

How old were these students?

This was college, but it felt more like junior high. Still, I encouraged more questions.

"How old are you?" was next, and the students gasped when they heard fifty-six.

I suppose I did look young compared to their grandmothers. They gasped again when they heard I had two grown sons and three grandchildren. Their faces were engaged, their eyes on me. I liked it up there. I began to tell them about why Woody and I had joined the Peace Corps, what the organization was about, how the Peace Corps was created in 1961 when I was only a few years younger than they were now.

And with that, the engaging eyes went blank. I faced silence and empty stares. So I turned it back to them.

"How about one more question?"

A hand went up near the front and I nodded to her. "What is Britney Spears like?"

"I have no idea," I sputtered. "I've never met her either."

Naively, I hadn't expected questions on pop culture. When I was their age, I had marched to stop the Vietnam War, end poverty, and fix civil rights forever. And the pop idols of my time were equally absorbed. I doubted these girls had ever heard of Bob Dylan or Joan Baez.

Their questions caught me off guard, when I'd expected to feel connected to them. And even worse: I kept expecting I'd have no expectations.

My thoughts raced as Raisa ended her class.

"Thank you, Janet," she said as a bell rang.

I followed her lead, gathered my rucksack, and we marched out the door.

When the morning classes were over, I walked back home to Symbat's, discouraged. I hoped the students of English 21—

whatever the 21 signified, I didn't yet know—weren't representative of the ones I'd teach. Were they not interested in world peace and cooperation, or was it that they knew so little English that I'd been wasting my breath? Worse, I didn't know which scenario I preferred.

These were second-year English majors and I expected them to understand English. I couldn't speak their language, certainly, whether Russian or Kazakh, and if they couldn't speak mine, how would we communicate? *What had I gotten myself into?*

I suddenly felt exhausted by the task ahead of me. And mad that, once again, my expectations could disappoint me so.

I would meditate, I decided, once I got home. In our little house on the water in Chincoteague, during the year before we left for the Peace Corps, I'd gotten into the habit of taking an hour each morning to read, to journal, and to sit quietly and empty my mind. But since we'd arrived in Kazakhstan, I hadn't once sat in meditation. I'd journalled, of course. But to sit quietly and do nothing—never mind trying to empty my mind—that I hadn't done. And I felt the difference.

Yes. That's what I'll do. I'd give myself half an hour, long enough to know again what was important.

When I got to the apartment, I called out a cheery "*Hello. Dobra d'yen,*" to Symbat, in the kitchen. Yeerasul at her feet, she carried on with her tasks as though she didn't hear me. *I must use the Kazakh hello.* But I kept forgetting it.

In the living room, Woody was slouched in an overstuffed chair, watching the 2004 Summer Olympics on TV.

"What's on?" I asked as I came in to say a quick hello, before meditating in the bedroom.

"Kazakh wrestling. I'm not sure who they're wrestling, though."

"In Kazakh or Russian?" I figured if it were Russian, I'd sit briefly, curious to see if I'd understand any of it. If Kazakh, I'd retreat to the bedroom.

"Kazakh, I think," he responded after a few moments hesitation and just after I'd plopped myself onto the overstuffed sofa.

But as I hit the cushion, a cold feeling of wet enveloped my bottom.

"Oooh!" I yelped, jumping up and hollering. "It's wet!"

Clearly, Yeerasul, the bare-bottomed toddler, had been there. I felt for the telltale sign.

"We've got to say something." I barked. I'd had enough surprises for one day.

"Good luck." Woody just smiled and went back to his television.

Imagining how my conversation with Symbat might go, I smiled, too, after a moment of breathing through my shock. If I used English, she wouldn't understand. To do it in Russian, I'd need our Russian-English dictionary, the one Woody had gifted to our previous host family. A new, more extensive one, a gift from his brother, wouldn't arrive for months—a reminder to get that post office box.

How to proceed? I wished I understood the absence of diapers better. Was this a financial issue or a child-raising philosophy? If I knew why Yeerasul didn't wear diapers, I assumed, it'd be easier to adapt. Not knowing how to address the situation, just as I'd found at my school that day, was troubling.

I went to the bedroom, eager for that half-hour of quiet meditation. But when I walked in, I found the floor strewn with the papers I'd brought with me from training. Handouts on one thing or another had been neatly arranged on the windowsill when I'd left that morning. And the window had been closed. Now it was open and I had a good twenty-minute job ahead of me to sort them out, if I really wanted to, which I didn't. Then my eye caught our new Toshiba laptop sitting on the table by the wall and I really got angry.

We'd spent nearly $3,000 to buy it, insure it, and have it shipped to us quickly before we left training. But we'd been unable to connect to the Internet in the apartment and no one seemed to know why. Now the expensive laptop was sitting there taunting me, reminding me of my powerlessness. Even the Word program it came with was temporary. I set about to pick up the papers. At least that was something I could fix.

Nariman came often, after dinner, to try get us connected.

"Nariman used to be a doctor," Zamzagul had told us the first evening, as Nariman fiddled with wires in a box on the wall. "But he likes fixing computers better."

I figured I'd missed something in Zamzagul's English. The second night they'd come over, we heard the problem hinged on the phone being on a party line. Finally, the explanation had to do with a bill the previous tenants had failed to pay before they turned the apartment over to Yergali, which had been the week we'd first moved in. In fact, we learned later, Yergali had rented this apartment because we'd be renting a room from him. This hadn't been their home, which helped explain its sparseness.

On some nights, while Nariman worked on getting the computer hooked up, Zamzagul talked to Yergali and Symbat in Kazakh. On other nights, she'd come without Nariman, but with Gulzhahan, and the four of them would sit in the living room, arguing. Again, we had no idea what was going on.

But on this night, after my frustrating day at school and my desire to just sit quietly at home was frustrated by my sense of overwhelm, as Nariman busied himself again with strange wires, Zamzagul made a surprise announcement.

"We've found another apartment for you. You will like it."

"Another apartment?" I was incredulous. Granted, life was grim where we were. We couldn't talk to either of our host parents—I got a kick out of calling them that, young as they were—and I was still quite sick from the raw herring Symbat had served the previous week. With Symbat's mother now sleeping on the sofa, it had gotten crowded. And, there were those wet spots in the living room.

But surely these were problems we could overcome. This was the Peace Corps, after all. There were supposed to be problems to overcome.

"Why?" I asked Zamzagul, simply.

"Yergali's brother is moving in," she said. "That will be too many people."

I wondered where he'd sleep, given that the mother-in-law already had the sofa. Suddenly, this crowded, oppressively silent home had become mine. We would figure out a solution. I had no intention of leaving.

"We can show you your new place tomorrow," Zamzagul added.

I didn't want to move. That was clear. I'd had enough newness; this strange family was at least familiar. Besides, to move before our six months was over seemed a huge failure. My cell phone cop-out was small potatoes in comparison.

Woody, though, had no reservations. "Anywhere would be better than here," he said when I tried to talk to him about it privately.

Again, I went along, agreeing to see the new apartment and to meet our new—our third—host family. I had no energy left to argue.

Chapter Eight
DINA

As a Peace Corps volunteer, I felt proud to represent my country. America is made up of a diverse collection of people, united in our liberty to not only hold different dreams, but to tread different paths to reach them.

I knew I couldn't represent all Americans, who come in different sizes, shapes, and colors. I could only be me. But, I was troubled that whatever I was, it wasn't going to be enough to make things work with Symbat and Yergali.

Life with Yergali and Symbat was particularly hard, maybe, because our experience with our first host family during our training had been so positive.

Our first host parents, Hadija and Mamluk, had four active teenagers that kept their big house alive. The two rooms that Woody and I shared were each larger than our bedroom at Symbat's. But it was more than the space. I'd enjoyed them. We'd enjoyed each other.

Hadija, who spoke no English, had taught me to make homemade noodles and strawberry jam; I'd taught her how to cook fried green tomatoes, French toast, and apple crisp. She would sit with us while we ate breakfast and talk to us using simple, easy-to-understand Russian words.

It was there at Hadija's table that I learned the two words for hot. I can still see her sitting on the bench across from us each morning, saying *zharka* and fanning her sweat-soaked forehead. *Garyachee*, she also taught us, is what the soup is when you have to blow on it.

And, she taught us the word for housefly, *mookha*, which I found similar enough to *moosh*, the Russian word for husband, to tease Woody. One of Hadija and Mamluk's daughters, Soniya, was learning English in school and served as a willing though shy translator. And they had a washing machine, something I took for granted until I was washing clothes in Symbat's bathtub. I missed them all very much.

Three days after Zamzagul told us we'd be moving, we were packed and ready to go. In recognition of our last day with her, Symbat prepared the national dish of Kazakhstan, *bishparmak*. I rolled the dough for the homemade noodles and then watched as she cooked them in the broth in which the meat had been simmering most of the morning.

Bishparmak is the dish for any special occasion, served on a large plate set in the middle of the table, not unlike a Thanksgiving turkey except that it's the only dish. The boiled meat, beef, mutton, or horse sits on a bed of homemade noodles with a thinly sliced onion and single shaved carrot for garnish. Vegetables aren't big in Kazakhstan.

Bizbarmak—the Kazakh spelling of *bishparmak*—is Kazakh for "five fingers," and, sure enough, just before the young men who would help us move arrived, we quietly ate from the central platter with our own five fingers.

Symbat's mother and husband were gone, off to jobs we never knew anything about. Eighteen-month-old Yeerasul sat on Symbat's lap, looking serene. Symbat was also quiet, her usual demeanor. Resignation, I suspected, was her primary characteristic.

"I will miss you," she said, her longest English sentence since we'd arrived, and I believed her.

I would miss her too, though, even after two weeks, I felt I hardly knew her. But I would wonder whether we might have felt at home there had we stayed and just tried harder.

When we were done with our meal, two of the anonymous young men, who had helped move us in two weeks before, returned to help us move out, and we rode off
to our new home in a taxi with much less ceremony than when we'd arrived.

✦

Because of the Peace Corps Kazakhstan policy that volunteers must spend their first nine months with a local family—our first three had been with Hadija—we were moving on to another host "family."

Dina Kurmanayeva was a thirty-eight-year-old divorced woman who taught English to future mining engineers at the university's college of mining engineering. Her apartment was right across from the *Akimat* (city hall), near Company Plus, the Internet café we'd been frequenting daily, and close to buses, taxis, shopping, and, in short, civilization.

As we rode the many blocks across town to our new apartment, Woody looked at me and complained.

"I don't know why Zamzagul didn't suggest this place in the beginning. Whose idea was it, anyway, to put us with someone that wouldn't speak Russian?"

Woody had been eager to move since the idea first arose. He hated the food that Symbat prepared, hated the lack of easy conversation, hated the hassles with the Internet, and mostly, just wanted to try something—anything—new.

I could only shrug. What could I say? I wasn't eager to move. But as our taxi carried us across town, I was resigned. I had my stiff upper lip in place and my all-is-well demeanor firmly fixed to cover what I saw as my second defeat, after cell phones.

85

We should have stuck it out ran repeatedly in my head, and, as we rode to our new home, I began to fixate on "what went wrong." How we had failed.

Our car pulled into a parking space in front of a nine-story cement-block building, tall for Zhezkazgan. The original elevator had long ago stopped working and we climbed to the fourth floor through a dark stairwell with that now-familiar urine-smelling, battered-mailbox ambiance.

Walking in, I noticed immediately that Dina's apartment was a real home. Mementos of her life, books, photos, trinkets, and souvenirs hung on the walls and lay on every available surface.

Dina greeted us warmly and showed us through the tiny three-room apartment. "You have the bedroom," she told us quickly, in English.

I noticed she'd already added a deadbolt lock on the bedroom door, in keeping with the Peace Corps' requirements. She wanted us.

Dina was tall, like Symbat, at maybe 5 feet 7 inches, with the shiny, short dark hair and the round Kazakh face I'd come to recognize as "not Russian." She had slanted Asian eyes and the high cheekbones I had associated with Native American Indians but now know go back to Mongol bloodlines.

I followed behind her, impressed at how friendly she was and all too aware she was speaking English. I wondered if Symbat would have also seemed friendlier had we spoken the same language.

"Where will you sleep?" I asked as we passed the small living room.

"Here," she said, indicating the three-cushion sofa.

And then I noticed the large wardrobe squeezed into one corner, next to the tiny TV and computer set on a typical computer stand.

I wandered into the kitchen to look out the window. Off in the distance, behind the university buildings across the street, I could see the body of water that Woody and I had stumbled upon during our first solo outing. I loved being able to see the water, whatever it was, and turned to him and smiled. I was glad we had moved; and I hated that I was glad.

Over our welcome meal of *bishparmak*—yes, when they call it the national dish, they mean *the* national dish—we settled on 14,000 *tenge* a month (just over $100) for the room and evening meals. This was 8,000 *tenge* (nearly $50) less than we had paid Symbat for the room and three meals a day. With this arrangement, Woody and I had the financial flexibility to eat out more often. We'd buy and fix our own breakfast and still stay within our Peace Corps budget, something I was still determined to do.

"What is your national dish?" Dina asked us as we ate, and appeared sad for us when we couldn't come up with just one.

"It depends on the region of the country you're from," I said, with Woody quickly adding, "And your ethnicity." *We can't even agree on this,* I thought, stifling a sudden burst of anger yet again. *I wish he'd just be quiet.*

One consequence of being an older volunteer was that Dina called me "mama." Of course, in Kazakhstan it was a good thing to be old enough to be her mother, if you don't mind having your age factor into how you are treated. I did.

Each time she called me "mama" I recoiled, missing my sons even more. She was not the daughter I'd never had and I resented her putting herself in that role. Then, I felt guilty for feeling so strongly about it.

Finally, I said something. "I wish you'd call me Janet," I told her one evening. Though she agreed, Dina found other ways to keep me in the parent role.

Like any "host mother," part of her responsibility was to fix us dinner every night. When I offered to help with the dishes after dinner, her reply was always a curt, "I will do it myself." And when I asked her to explain, she'd say only, "It is the daughter's job." I wanted to scream.

It wasn't too much later that I came to understand why having a "mama" in the house was so important to her. Dina's parents were deceased. Her father had died of lung disease at forty-nine, the consequence of his work in the nearby mines. And, one evening when I arrived home to find her standing at her stove, frying clumps of dough, I learned about the loss of her mother. And the death of her only child.

"This is God bread," she told me quietly as I stared at the stack of flat pieces of bread dough she'd just fried. "We make it to honor someone."

Then, having put the remaining pieces on the stack and turning off the burner, she pulled out a chair at the small kitchen table and motioned for me to join her. She had something to say.

"Tomorrow it will be nine years," she began.

I sat quietly, seeing she was having some difficulty speaking.

"Nine years ago my daughter was killed in the street."

I swallowed my horror as Dina continued.

"And my mother, too."

I listened as Dina told the story of the car that had struck her mother and her only child, just five years old, as they walked hand-in-hand across a nearby street.

"My mother died immediately," she said, "but my daughter died at the hospital." .

"I'm so sorry," was all I could say.

I wanted to touch her hand, but I held back, concerned she would find it intrusive. I asked about her daughter.

"What was her name?" I began.

But Dina couldn't tell me. Her voice shook and she worked so hard to hold back her tears. Still struggling with such an enormous loss, she held on tight to the tears she needed to shed.

I urged her to cry, telling her how crying often helped me. But she would have none of it.

"My marriage," she continued. "He wouldn't stay. This should be my wedding anniversary." And, in a final blow, the day after would have been her daughter's birthday.

Then, as if she had spoken of too much of what was ill, she wanted me to know that it wasn't the driver's fault.

"Did he stop?" I asked.

"They were walking in the street," she explained. "They shouldn't have been." And she took a long, slow breath. "The driver was kind," she insisted. "He gave me money at the funeral."

But when I asked about an investigation, Dina looked at me blankly.

"We make *shelpak* for such occasions. God bread," she said, changing the subject back to the flat circles of fried dough she had been making. "Always an uneven number. Even numbers are for happy times."

Woody and I ate dinner alone that night, the dinner Dina had prepared for us, and she went to her brother's home, to the family that is always at the center of any occasion, festive or sad.

Chapter Nine
ON TOWARD MY MELTDOWN

The late September weather was a combination of October mornings and August afternoons. With humidity nearly nonexistent, the weather was, for me, the best thing about Kazakhstan. My raw herring-induced "Genghis Khan's Revenge" had finally subsided, but the head-cold-turned-laryngitis I'd been fighting for over a week was getting worse, and my fatigue seemed never to end.

Stepping outside of Dina's apartment each morning, I pulled my sweater around me against the morning chill, and rechecked my wad of menthol-infused tissues, determined to carry on.

Since we'd arrived, several local holidays—Miners' Day, Constitution Day, Knowledge Day, the Day for Oil and Gas Workers, and a Day for Nuclear Industry Workers—had come and gone with barely any notice. Then, on October 1, with me feeling not at all like celebrating, Teachers' Day rolled around.

"Don't forget the party tonight," Gulzhahan reminded me one afternoon as I was collecting my long-forgotten sweater, ready to go home after school. "It's for the teachers. You must come."

I nodded noncommittally; I was planning to stay home and rest but didn't want to tell her. I wasn't in the mood for a party. But when three of my colleagues arrived at Dina's apartment that evening to escort me to the event, I was touched enough to change my mind. I would try to forget I was in the throes of the worst head cold of my memory and try instead to spend a relaxing evening with my colleagues. Stiff upper lip, check.

We walked the half a mile or so to the party center, found the party was still being set up, and settled into a corner with comfortable seats and into easy conversation, in Kazakh of course, but with enough English that I didn't feel ignored. Soon, other teachers from our department joined us and I pulled out my digital camera, eager to capture their faces.

It was always hard to get a candid photo in Kazakhstan for, as soon as people saw my camera, they posed with wide grins on their faces practically cheerleader-pyramid-style, climbing on chairs in back, sliding underneath whomever was in front, or poking a head in between two others. I'd found that if I took enough of these posed photos, everyone would eventually settle back into natural routines and forget about my lens and me, and I could get the candid shots I wanted.

The party got under way an hour after we arrived, and we moved to the table assigned to the English department. Set for twelve and identical to the other tables, ours had the requisite salad plate, shot glass, wine glass, and water glass at each place. We even had forks as well as spoons. We'd eaten with spoons at all of the homes we'd been in.

Perched identically on every table, at opposite corners of each, were bottles of brandy, vodka, and red wine. There was also a box of juice and a bottle of mineral water. Each table would have at least one man whose job it was to make certain everyone's glasses remained full. Since our table held only female teachers, a waiter would pour ours.

In Kazakhstan, insisting that you eat and drink is part of the host's responsibility and a matter of honor. Alcohol flowed freely with the expectation that everyone would partake in every toast.

Before dinner, I'd turned my shot glass upside down, at Gulzhahan's suggestion, and had no hassle over drinks. I noticed that most of my colleagues left theirs full and sipped occasionally, also with no hassles.

But one of our English teachers emptied hers often. Each time, our very attentive male stand-in refilled it immediately. As her speech slurred and her volume and verbosity increased, the other teachers distanced themselves from her, until I, sitting next to her, remained the only one left nodding to her.

Déjà vu. I'd known enough drunks with whom I'd tried to maintain the illusion of having an actual conversation, placating them so they wouldn't get angry. I'd expected never to put myself in that position again. Yet, here I was. I wanted to go home. Tired, sick, and hot before, now I was really miserable.

"Gulzhahan, can I leave? I don't want to insult anyone."

"No, it isn't time," she gently replied.

I'd wait; she had yet to steer me wrong.

Later that night, when I slipped outside to cool off, I saw just how seriously Gulzhahan took her responsibilities as head of the English teachers.

It was dark out, the moon just a thin curl, and the lights of the party center didn't cover the full courtyard. I could hear Gulzhahan though, in an unlit corner of the patio and nearly out of sight, giving our inebriated teacher a chewing-out—in Kazakh, of course—but a chewing-out is a chewing-out, no matter what language.

I wished I hadn't heard it, but I'd had to get away from the heat inside the building. I'd worn my standard camisole with my long-sleeved green knit top over it, a combination that had served me well over the years when menopause was rearing its hot-flashy head and I was unsure how hot I'd be. But I hadn't considered the camisole in the context of a room full of Muslim men and women. Granted, these were alcohol-drinking Muslim men and women, but still.

I'd asked Gulzhahan during dinner, "Can I take this off?" showing her the camisole underneath and expecting her to grant me permission.

"No. It's better," she'd answered; so I left it on. I was stuck. And, forgiveness being easier to get than permission, I was sorry I'd asked.

Back at our table, I tried to ignore my discomfort by focusing on the after-dinner game now in progress. Three men and one woman lined up to toss a ring over the neck of a bottle of wine. The winner would get the wine. I noticed that the director, who was running the game, was picking up the ring and setting it over the neck of the bottle each time one particular player missed. And everyone, even the other three players, laughed and went along with it. I asked Gulzhahan about it.

"He is our new teacher," she told me, by way of sufficient explanation.

It reminded me of playing board games with my sons when they were young. How often I'd give one an answer if he seemed to be lagging behind, or let them win at checkers if they'd been on a losing streak. When playing games, it always seemed necessary to retain the element of play.

After the game, we danced. A group of women gathered on the floor and I eagerly joined in as they formed a circle, dancing to a song with a strong beat. With the soaring temperatures in the room, my head fuzzy, and my body aching, I put it all out of my mind and enjoyed dancing solo within the larger group.

Committed to having fun, I be-bopped around to my own inner drummer for a bit, but soon enough noticed the other teachers in our circle were watching me, staring even. I paid them no mind. As the song says, I dance like nobody's watching. They could stare all they wanted.

But then I noticed one teacher biting her lower lip as she danced. I bite my lower lip when I dance. So, I stopped biting my lip. She stopped, too. I took my right arm and made a large circle overhead. The teachers in our group now made large circles overhead with their right arm. I bit my lip again and sure enough, they followed suit. Oh, my! Did they think I was modeling some popular American dance?

94

"There's some mistake here," I wanted to cry out, self-conscious. "I'm doing nothing special. Really."

But I didn't say a word. Glad to be part of the group, I kept dancing, and they kept imitating me. I was hot, I was tired, but I was okay. And I won the first dance contest, for the same reason, I'm sure, that the tall young teacher won the bottle toss. Perhaps it was their sense of duty, honor, obligation, or fun. It was certainly not for my skill.

My prize, a velvet Kazakh vest, identical in style to the one I got on my birthday, but this one a deep shade of blue, was a gift disguised as a prize. I didn't have to earn it. Earning it would have been so American.

I was pleased to rest a bit after the dance ended, and I could see they were setting the stage for another game. I stood up, hoping to get outside again and cool off. But as I stood, I heard the director call my name.

"*DZANET*," he called too loudly, followed by something in Kazakh. The older Kazakh matrons, probably more assistant directors, were motioning me to join the two women teachers standing in the middle of the dance floor. With them were the director and two male teachers. It appeared it was my turn to play a game.

Gulzhahan came up with me, to translate, I thought, and stood behind my left shoulder. The other women and I were paired with the men, who were each standing on a chair facing out while we three women stood in front, facing them at what I immediately saw was a most unfortunate height. I was paired with the director, whose crotch was now at eye level.

Gulzhahan leaned over to talk to me softly. She was not actually translating; she was speaking directly to me. It was hard to hear her in the din of the room, but her words were clear. "You don't have to do this. You don't have to do this."

"I'm okay. I want to play," I told her. How bad could it be?

The game seemed simple enough. We each were to push a ping-pong ball up our partner's pant leg, across his crotch, and down the other side. Easy, too. But as it dawned on me what I had to do, I glanced up at the man who had given me creepy glances during my formal introduction. I did not want to be intimate with his crotch. I gave a quick nod to my Puritan forefathers who obviously hadn't ever landed in Kazakhstan.

This was not what the Peace Corps meant by wanting us to get to know the people and the culture of our host country. Nor was it what they meant in those ads about, "The hardest job you'll ever love."

So many thoughts flitted through my head. But I was there to do a job, to do that job well, to be liked by my peers, and to have my country liked because of it. I'd sooner dig a latrine than play this game of ball-across-the-crotch-of-a-creepy-guy but, just like the thousands of Peace Corps volunteers before me had said, I could do it if I had to.

Gulzhahan tried one more time. "You don't have to do this," then fell silent when I waved her off. I would do it because I wanted them to like me. Classic co-dependency, but hindsight hadn't shown up yet.

I placed the ping-pong ball under the director's right cuff and started to pinch it upward, pulling the pant material as far from his skin as possible. In no time, I was at his knee. I could feel his eyes on the top of my head and imagined his lascivious leer. But then, before I knew it, I was at the top of his leg.

One of my competitors was already on her way over to the second pant leg. My thoughts were a jumble. *What if I touch the damned thing!* I'd been in nursing school for a year giving bed baths to prostate cancer patients; I'm the mother of two sons; I'm married, for heaven's sake, twice. Still, I didn't want to give the creepy director the satisfaction.

In I plunged, maneuvering the ping-pong ball across to his left pant leg and then dropping it into my right hand at his cuff. But my hesitancy had cost me valuable seconds and I came in third. The others must have had more practice. Or more alcohol. *Thank God it was over.*

The memory of the game lingered for days, haunting me. Guilt at participating in something that felt lewd—in public no less—and disgust at the director's leering expression, plagued me. Anger at the people who would even consider inviting an unsuspecting foreigner to join in was countered by anger at myself for not listening to Gulzhahan—she always steered me right—then anger at myself for being prudish, for not having more of an open mind.

Was my culture really so repressed that I, a sophisticated woman of the world, could still feel scandalized? But then again, wasn't this game nothing more than sexism wrapped up neatly as jocularity and playfulness? What was I thinking by agreeing to participate?

My feelings over the next few days also grew into a big jumble. When I talked to Woody, his attempts to empathize left me feeling even more emotionally isolated than ever. He wanted me to explain my feelings to him and I couldn't. I wanted only for him to just know what I needed. I wanted him to anticipate that when I was as miserable as I was, he was supposed to fix it.

"You don't do husband well." I snapped at him one evening. "You were a great boyfriend, but you've gotta get the husband bit down better."

With that, he left me alone.

I was sick of being tired, and I was tired of being sick. Something would soon have to give.

And it did.

Chapter Ten
THE MELTDOWN

Gulzhahan had helped me set up a post office box a few weeks before the ping-pong ball game, and Woody and I finally received the new dictionary from his brother in Canada. In short order we also got our boxes of "non-essentials" that the Peace Corps staff had had each volunteer pack up before we flew out of Washington DC, and the first of many fully loaded care packages from my seventy-something-year-old mother in Pennsylvania.

Stopping by the *pochta*—calling the post office by its Russian word made me feel more bilingual—on my way home from school became my custom.

"*Vosim desit, pajalsta,*" (number eighteen, please), I would say to the nearest *pochta* woman, then add, "*stoneyboot?*" (anything?). In less than a week, the staff was getting my mail before I uttered a word.

That fall, my two youngest grandchildren turned one year old. Sad to miss their special birthdays, I needed to reassure myself that my sons would know I was with them in spirit.

My search for the perfect gifts ended with two tiny Russian *shapkas*: sheepskin hats with the fur on the inside. One in dark leather that looked like an early airplane pilot cap would go to Dave's son, Elijah. The other was lighter, a pure sheepskin color, and would go to Jon's daughter, Isabella. The earflaps on both clinched it, so cute in those tiny sizes.

I wrapped them in a sturdy cardboard box, addressed it to David since he and his brother lived in the same town and, since he worked out of his home, would be available to receive the gifts when they were delivered. But I had no tape to secure the package.

I assumed the *pochta* ladies would give me some, like they would at my post office in Chincoteague, and went there expecting a simple process: add tape, fill out triplicate customs forms, pay money, leave. How easy it was to forget that even the most mundane activities might be done differently.

In Kazakhstan, the customer doesn't wrap the packages, the *pochta* employee does. I thought this a nice gesture. Perhaps, coming out of such poverty as they were, most people couldn't afford to buy the boxes or wrapping paper. I was wrong.

I brought the hats neatly wrapped in the perfect-sized cardboard box, and asked for the tape. I could see it on the shelf behind where the-woman-who-deals-with-packages stood, and pointed right at it.

"*Ya hachoo eta,*" (I want that), I said clearly in my most humble voice, adding "*Pajalsta*" (please) to be sure not to offend.

"*Nyet, nyet,*" she responded, though not quite so succinctly. I got the gist.

She spoke less English than I spoke Russian, but I finally understood she couldn't mail the box with tape. Tape was not allowed. Packages had to have, of all things, string.

In my halting Russian I pleaded, "If it has string, someone in America will open it and steal the contents."

At least I tried to say this. I got no response. She turned to wait on another customer, leaving me with my triplicate copies of the customs forms to fill out.

"If it has string," I yelled after her, in mixed Russian-English, "the string will get caught in the American machines. The box will be ripped apart." I was frantic. I had to get my presents mailed in a way that would get them there intact. I had to make this woman understand. I had to make her know how the American postal system worked. *They could learn a thing or two from the American postal system.*

Another *pochta* woman came over and added, "*Vui v'Kazakhstan, nyet* USA." (You're in Kazakhstan, not the USA.)

"But it's going to the USA," I offered, using a gesture that surely looked like a package crossing the ocean. I thought I was quite clear. But I could feel my face getting red, my voice rising to that "too loud" stage that hits just as other people start to notice. And a lump in my throat began to form.

Lady number two yelled back again, "*Vui v'Kazakhstan seechas.*" (You're in Kazakhstan now), and handed me a note with 1,542 written on it.

Defeated, I paid the 1,542 *tenge* (not even $12, but my remaining spending allowance for the entire month) and handed her my now filled-in triplicate customs form and walked out, expecting never to see the cute little *shapkas* again, certainly not on my grandchildren's heads.

Outside the post office, I fumed. They were right; I was in Kazakhstan now. And I was devastated.

The hassle at the post office wasn't merely a stumble for me. It was a crash, face first, so hard it knocked my breath away. Crushed by the possibility that I would not have a presence at my grandchildren's first birthday, I tried to reassure myself that my sons would understand and my grandchildren wouldn't even notice. But it wasn't enough.

Woody found my *pochta* story entertaining and was impressed that I'd even tried to mail the package alone, admitting he wouldn't have. But the pain I felt in how it had turned out was mine alone. And alone, I bore the grief. And worse, I bore it silently.

My simmering depression didn't hit me all at once the way Genghis Khan's revenge had, nor did it come on like the laryngitis that had built slowly but steadily into the worst head cold of my life.

Instead, it waxed and waned over the next few weeks. When it waned, life was good enough; the days passed by as if I were in a trance. When it waxed, the everyday events of my life took on a strange new dimension.

I began to have difficulty waking up each morning, felt tired constantly, and found myself feeling more alone than I'd felt since the years before my divorce. Everything seemed out of proportion and my tolerance for frustration was nil—classic signs of depression, all, and I failed to recognize a single one.

One cold and dark early October morning, before I learned it was faster to walk to work—warmer too, with arms swinging and papers tucked in the rucksack on my back—I joined about twenty people waiting for a bus.

The people at the stop were always a grim but docile enough crowd while they waited. But once the bus arrived, they'd surge forward *en masse*, leaving no room for the meek. I generally didn't care if I got on last because I was not on long enough to need a seat.

That Monday morning, with my frustration level past the saturation point, things turned out quite differently. When the bus arrived, I waited as usual while the crowd surged forward. But before I could squeeze on, the door closed and the bus began to rumble away.

On other mornings, this was the point when the fare collector might see me and get the driver to stop the bus. But this time, as I stepped off the curb to wave to her, the Number 5 bus, one I didn't want, pulled into the curb, sending me leaping backwards out of its way in fear for my life.

I darted behind the interloper bus, rounding its backside in time to see my Number 3 pull away, its fare collector nowhere to be seen. I would be late to class and I snapped. The tension I'd been barely containing for weeks came flooding out of me.

Running to the front of Number 5, I banged my fists on the driver's door window.

"I missed my bus, thanks to you!" I screamed in English, "Now what am I supposed to do? What were you thinking?" I added a few expletives, too, basking in the sudden sense of power I felt at using the forbidden words.

He stared complacently at me through his window and slowly pulled away.

What was I thinking?

I walked back to the sidewalk, defeated. Rather than realizing I needed to take some time to get my head together—a bubble bath had helped me during an earlier, smaller version of this at Hadija's during training—I just stood there, determined that the next time I'd use my elbows to get aboard, as the others did.

I was Anakin Skywalker going over to the dark side. I would not let anyone, even the elderly or infirm, cut in front of me again. The injustice of it made me crazy—a crazy foreigner who said she was there to make friends for America.

At least my explosion at the bus stop was among strangers and I could blend quickly back into anonymity. But later that week, another low point hit me while I was sitting in the teachers' lounge. My witnesses were my colleagues.

The day was cold outside and the chill seeped through the walls. The teachers had been talking about the upcoming election.

"Things here will never change," one of them said.

As though on cue, something deep within me burst. "With an attitude like that, it's no wonder!" I snapped.

I knew immediately I shouldn't have said it. At best, I'd said something rude, and, at worst, something intentionally insulting.

But none of the teachers in the small room reacted. There was not even an uncomfortable silence. It wasn't a language barrier issue. There simply wasn't an aggressive bone in any of them. I wanted to scream; I wanted them to be angry, angry with me, just like I was.

Deep in my genetic code, there was a belief that any problem could be at least addressed if not fixed. No mountain too high, no ocean too deep, yadda, yadda, yadda. But in Kazakhstan, I found no ethic that said if the system is broken, it should get fixed. And what was even harder for me, I rarely heard anyone acknowledge that anything in the system was broken.

From where I stood that particular gloomy day, everything I saw was broken. From the women rifling through my grandchildren's birthday presents, to teachers pushing a ping-pong ball up some stranger's pant leg, to the scene at the bus stop. I was tired of dealing with behaviors I didn't like, never mind understand.

I was worn out by the terrible bleakness all around me. I was irritated by eating when not hungry only because whoever offered the food might be offended if I didn't. I was sick of drinking tea so full of the caffeine that wreaked havoc with my sleep. I was tired of trying to believe none of it mattered. In short, I was tired of being culturally sensitive.

I badly needed someone who would just listen to me, help me see things in perspective, laugh with me. Bakhit, the woman at my college whom I'd thought might become my first friend, had never again showed any interest in me. And Tatiana, a woman for whom I held out much hope for friendship during my first month in Zhezkazgan, had moved to Moscow the week after we'd met.

I'd lost Woody, too, as far as I was concerned. I was disappointed that he couldn't cheer me up, that he never brought me broth when I was sick unless I asked him, that I had to ask him. I was annoyed at constantly tripping over his stuff in our tiny room and angry that when I tried to share my struggles with him, he didn't understand.

I worried whether I even knew my husband at all. We'd once been so close. Perhaps we'd been too close—like standing before a tree or a mirror, so close you can't see either the forest or the face. Now that I'd stepped back a bit, I wasn't seeing what I expected to see. And the distance between us felt immense.

How much easier my adjustment would have been, I decided, if the Peace Corps had placed me in Africa or the South Pacific. With different clothing, an occasional loincloth at least, the visual reminders that I was in a different culture would surely have made my adjustment easier.

In Kazakhstan, the cultural differences were enormous, yet they were subtle, often out of sight. People looked like Americans, wore American clothing, had American hairstyles. The differences that were knocking me over were hidden from view. And, things I normally did on automatic pilot, I now had to think about.

I couldn't walk through a doorway without a conscious, "I must pick up my feet." I couldn't enter a home without going through the very conscious ritual of removing my shoes, a literal "rite of passage." I didn't mind removing my shoes. I liked the custom in many ways. What I minded was the thinking about it. I was on hyper-alert all day long, every day, and I was exhausted.

I pictured myself sitting by a pool, with a gorgeously tanned and well-muscled man with a flirtatious smile serving me an ice-cold margarita, a curious image, given that I don't tend to enjoy pools. Pure luxury, that's what I longed for, and a little relaxation. A respite.

❧

I hit my metaphorical bottom a few days after I blew up at my colleague. After picking up a package with photos of my grandchildren, I sat on the cement wall outside the *pochta,* that clear no-no in this land of superstitions, to open it. But on this particular day, as I sat on the wall, no old woman ran over to me, insisting I stand up. Probably my loud sobbing kept them all at bay.

Tired of pushing my sadness away, tired of fighting it, I finally accepted that the only way around this difficult time was to go through it. "The only way around is through" was a mantra that had helped me through the painful years leading up to my divorce.

I'd spouted the adage over the previous ten years in workshops and various keynote addresses, in the textbook Woody and I wrote together, and with my clients in my psychotherapy practice.

"The only way around is through," I repeated to myself now, and knew it was time to sit still and feel my feelings.

"Courage," another adage I'd often quoted, is "feeling the fear and doing it anyway." Now was the time for me to face up to my own fear *du jour* and push forward, confronting what I'd been afraid of, embracing my inner demons, if you will. I wanted my Peace Corps years to be good ones, my time worth all I'd left behind. I wanted to be happy again. That much I knew.

I thought of the yoga teacher I'd had throughout the early 1980s. Larry Terkel had taught me to find my "point of resistance" and "play with it." His advice had been vital a decade later as I came out of my stuttering closet, finding that moment when I was stuttering and just staying with it, not being in such a hurry to get away. No more numbing out, no more excuses.

Sitting on the cement wall outside the Zhezkazgan post office, I'd do it again. I'd honor my "point of resistance," feel my sadness, and stretch and pull it all I could.

My sobs helped. I sobbed through my embarrassment that I, the certified Gestalt psychotherapist, had been stuffing my feelings and numbing out to the many disappointments I'd found. And I sobbed through my dismay that I, the Master of

Arts sociologist, had been seeing this culture through my own ethnocentric filter, wearing a sun visor of "my way" that colored everything I saw, judging the new by what I knew.

I sobbed for the discriminating eye that had served me well in so many arenas back home in my own culture, but that was wreaking havoc on me in Kazakhstan. And I sobbed through the denial that had convinced me I'd feel fine if only I gritted my teeth, stepped up, and plowed on.

I sobbed through the frustrations and the anger of the past months: the institutionalized chaos that stopped me short on a daily basis, the neglect that surrounded me wherever I looked, and the dust that covered me with every step. And I sobbed away my disappointment in Woody, and my fear, believing that if we weren't destined for the "happy ever after" I'd expected, I'd still be okay.

Mostly, I sobbed into my acknowledgment that I couldn't control any of it. I leaned into my crying eagerly, hungrily, knowing as sure as I knew my name, that crying "clears away the sadness and creates a space for joy."

When my sobbing had run its course, I blew my nose, wiped my face, and recognized a long-lost sense of excitement. I felt the eager anticipation of the unknown as I once had the night before leaving for a new summer camp, the days before a new school year began, or the weeks before each of my sons was born.

With renewed energy, I walked home, eager to share my metamorphosis with Woody. Hoping, too, that I'd no longer be so constantly angry with him.

I'd climbed that high dive for Woody in the beginning, then jumped off it for the stories I could tell my grandchildren about "making friends for America." The resultant fall—where I'd been—had seemed endless. But once I hit, there on that post office wall, I knew the rest of my time in Kazakhstan would be categorically different.

I was there for me now, and the fact that I had no idea exactly how the rest of my time there would be different, was OK. I just knew it would be.

PART II

We have to continually be jumping off cliffs and developing our wings on the way down.
Kurt Vonnegut (1922-2007)

Chapter Eleven
MUDDY WATERS

"The trick," cultural anthropologist Gregory Bateson once said, "is to know which differences make a difference." In the days and weeks after my cry on the post office wall, the myriad differences surrounding me began to fade.

They were all still there: the chaos and neglect, the rudeness of the people on the street, the undercurrent of graft, and the overtly patriarchal system that even the women seemed to buy into. But now I tried a new tack. I would observe first, judge last. I would try to stand in that muddy middle I so disliked, that place between black and white, good and bad, right and wrong. Who knew. Maybe I'd get to like it there.

One afternoon, back at the *pochta,* while I waited to collect my mail, a woman pushed in front of me out of the amorphous crowd. *Why did no one take turns?* I'd been asking myself that question since we first landed in Kazakhstan. Now, with my curiosity rekindled, I set about on a new path. Whatever mail I had would be there whether I was next in line or tenth, so I stepped out of the line I thought I was in to watch the crowd.

Hugging the wall, I let my gaze float over the dozen or so Kazakhstanis huddled in the open area between the door and the teller-type windows. Nothing stood out to me except that others were also getting pushed aside. I felt myself getting that old familiar frustration.

Then, someone new came through the doors and I heard him call out, "*Kto posledny?*" I had no idea what that meant, but in response I noticed a faint murmuring in the crowd. A few heads nodded toward someone standing off to the side and I saw him nod in acknowledgment.

"*Kto posledny*," it turned out, was the equivalent of "Who's at the end of the line?" I'd never heard the question before, never mind answering it. For all anyone knew, I'd been the one pushing ahead in line. How quick I'd been to criticize something I knew so little about.

Another epiphany came to me at school. Personal space—how far away one must stand when talking to someone face-to-face—is a common cultural difference, and I'd arrived ready to give up my habitual thirty inches. I never had to, though, since Kazakhs stand generally where Americans stand when talking to each other.

What had consistently surprised me, however, was seeing young women draped over each other while sitting in class, girls and young women walking down the street hand in hand, and women greeting each other with a kiss on the lips. None of this had to do with sexual orientation, our Peace Corps trainers were quick to emphasize. Still, I'd found it disquieting at first.

On one particular day, somewhere in late October, as my English teacher colleagues gathered in the conference room on the first floor and two of our teachers curled up together on a small sofa against the wall, I noticed I was having a new reaction. The more I watched them, the more inviting their closeness looked to me.

There in Kazakhstan, sitting around the long conference table with my fellow teachers that October morning, listening to yet another assistant director complaining about something I didn't understand, the idea of a pair of comforting arms around me was appealing.

Physical contact has become sexualized in my culture, I knew—probably another gift of our Puritan forefathers. But what I saw among my fellow teachers wasn't sexual; it was pure comfort. Their freedom to snuggle with someone in public, with no one thinking it odd as they appreciated the sheer physicality of it brought me a surprising sense of envy.

How lucky they were.

Along with feminist author Gloria Steinem and *Jonathan Livingston Seagull's* Richard Bach, I believe that "we teach what we need to learn." The Russians have an easy way to remember this: they use the same word, *uchitele*, for both "I teach" and "I learn." At least it was the same to my ear. In any case, I found many opportunities to *uchitele* in my classrooms.

As a matter of course, most of my students sat quietly, afraid to speak unless they knew they'd answer correctly, perfectly. I could empathize, of course. From the moment of my first grade reading circle through my high school English classes and up to the child psychology course I never took in college because it required a formal presentation, I knew how powerful the fear of public speaking could be. Too often when I tried to speak and the words "stuck," people responded by snickering. I eventually understood that they didn't mean to be mean, they just didn't know any better. But more importantly, I'd also learned that the more I gave in to my fear, the stronger it got.

Now, as a teacher, I would try to pass on to these "shy" students the idea that perfectionism can lead to a kind of paralysis that stops us from experiencing life, that messiness and mistakes have value, and, as I'd so recently rediscovered, that usually the best way past something we're afraid of is to plow right through it.

"Learning a new language is like learning to walk," I would tell all my classes near the beginning of our classroom

113

relationship. "We have to fall down at first. And, if we are lucky, we'll be able to laugh when we do."

While Woody was teaching English grammar and English literature from established texts at his university, though to very small classes of only three or four students, I needed to find my own materials and create my own topics for nearly 150 students in my seven different classes. This was all new territory for me, and I found it unexpectedly exciting.

During training, the Peace Corps had introduced us to small group work and games, geared to those students who were less afraid to speak aloud. But I wanted all my students to participate, even the "shy" ones. Since it's well known in the stuttering literature that people who stutter don't stutter when speaking in chorus, I thought perhaps the same trick could be used with my silent students. So, I added a few recitation-in-unison exercises to enable all the students who showed up to participate, even the shy ones.

Reciting-in-unison allowed me be silly, something the students seemed to particularly enjoy. I used arm movements to direct my students, keeping them together in their chorusing. This worked well with teaching the days of the week.

"Monday, Tuesday, Wednesday," the class would chorus with me as I walked up and down the aisles, arms circling in a slow, gentle rhythm. I kept my eyes on the silent students toward the back of the room. When I found one not participating, I'd bend down close to her so she could hear my voice. "Thursday, Friday, Saturday," I would say, and, through the smile on my face, dare her to join in. If she didn't, I'd continue to smile as I went on, "Sunday, Monday, Tuesday." Eventually she would catch on.

After the whole class caught the rhythm, I could speed them up or slow them down by changing the speed of my arms. And, even more fun, if the class was following well, I'd change the direction of my arms and dare them to recite the words backwards. "Friday, Thursday, Wednesday," was always accompanied by much giggling.

The first time I did this, I felt the joy of victory. I'd gotten them to plow through their fear, and I could see the joy on their faces as they did so.

You see, I wanted to yell, *you can do this!*

❀

Because I was still "*uchitel*-ing" my way, I tried to incorporate exploration of culture into language lessons whenever I could think of a way to do so. These lessons tied something I wanted to learn to something my students could teach me, using English. One of our first ones was about Kazakh families.

My English 39 class was a particularly shy group of students, so I introduced the topic of families by taping a poster of my own genogram on the blackboard. Circles represented women and squares represented men. For my family, seven squares and five circles covered four generations.

"I am an only child," I began, pointing to the solitary circle with my name and birth date in the center.

I introduced my parents as my finger followed the vertical lines connecting me to my mother's circle and my father's square. Each had his or her names and birth dates, and for my father, his death date as well. Moving up, I introduced my two sets of grandparents.

I continued my explanation by running my finger to the right from my circle where I pointed to a square and explained, "This is Woody, my husband."

Then, I pointed to the square to the left of my circle. "And this is my first husband, Martin, my sons' father."

I went on explaining the relationships between my circle and the shapes for my children and my grandchildren.

"Where are your brothers and sisters?" one student asked.

115

"I don't have any."

Murmurs and gasps wafted up and down the rows of desks. But when I added that I had no aunts or uncles either, that my mother was also an only child, the murmurs and gasps turned to giggles and shouts of "no!"

I must have seemed very alien to these students, all of whom came from large families.

"Martin, my sons' father, is also an only child," I said. They were learning a new English term: only child.

I then handed out paper, passed around crayons, and gave them time to create their own family trees, which they would present at our next class.

Kazakhs know their paternal lineage back at least seven generations. But I also noted that while every one of my twenty-six students knew their paternal grandfathers' name, only one knew the name of her maternal grandmother.

Culture is so often reflected in language—and vice versa, some would say—and their paternal focus is indeed reinforced in their language. The Kazakh words *apa* (grandmother) and *ata* (grandfather) refer only to the father's parents. There is no special word for the parent of a mother. *Nagashi apa*, which translates loosely as "mother's relative" is all there is.

I was shocked. But then my students explained to me that they preferred to visit their mothers' relatives where they'd be "treated as a guest." When they visited their fathers' parents, "it is like family," they said. "We must work."

Their laughter helped ease my dismay.

Some of my students also talked openly and easily of being raised by grandparents or aunts and uncles. No particular tragedy had stolen their parents away. Rather, my students insisted, it showed how large their real family was. Their parents may have had many children and a beloved uncle or aunt had none. The nuclear family, so central to Western families in the post-World War II years, appeared to be one more Western creation often taken as a universal.

My resistance to the patriarchal nature of the system notwithstanding, I had to admit that these extended Kazakh families enjoyed a closeness that made the typical American nuclear family—never mind my own tiny one—seem rather isolated in comparison.

✤

Peace Corps likes to emphasize that cultural exchange goes in two directions, and our first Thanksgiving gave us an opportunity to act on this.

We planned to host a typical American holiday with Dina. I'd been so focused on adapting to Kazakh culture that I welcomed the chance, however small, to focus on inviting others into my cultural traditions. And Thanksgiving is my favorite holiday. We set out to find a turkey.

"We call it *induk*," Dina told us, which is also the Russian word for India.

"That's interesting," declared Woody, who then proceeded to tell us how the Dutch word for turkey, *kalkoen* (like Calcutta), and the French, *dindon*, also show a belief that the turkey hails from India.

Wherever it hails from, there were no *induks* at any of the markets. So, we put out feelers to my 148 students, Woody's ten or so, both our counterparts, and anyone else we could collar. Although Gulzhahan assured me there were *induks* to be found in Kazakhstan, after a full week of disappointing leads, I began to have doubts.

With only ten days before our celebration, we awoke to good news from Dina.

"Gulzhahan has found your turkey," she said one morning at breakfast.

It seemed that after all our dead ends, Gulzhahan had seen a TV advertisement for turkeys long after we'd gone to bed. She

117

called the number, then called Dina to give her the news. I was excited. But as the week went on, we engaged in an odd conversation through Dina with the turkey seller, and my excitement took different turns.

"How much does a turkey cost?" We put our first question to Dina.

The price was not cheap, almost $30.

"How big is it?" We were afraid it might be too big to fit inside Dina's tiny electric oven.

"They don't know." Dina told us. "They said they can't just pop one up on a scale. The turkeys are alive. They don't hold still long enough."

Alive? We hadn't even considered they'd be alive.

With just one week left before Thanksgiving, we decided that, even with all the effort put into finding this turkey by so many people, we'd have to pass. Substituting a roast chicken wouldn't work as meat displays contained only the dark meat double joints. We decided that we'd serve *bishparmak* at our international Thanksgiving instead.

But Dina, bless her heart, didn't stop looking. She searched the city until she found someone who would slaughter our turkeys for us. Yes, turkeys. Having learned they were small, Dina had ordered two.

Three days before Turkey-Day, Woody, Dina, and I found ourselves in a car at about 8 o'clock at night. Where the car came from and who was driving was a mystery to me then and remains a mystery to me today. Off we all went to pick up our live turkeys. Woody held one on his lap in a cardboard box in the front seat while I held the second one in a cloth bag on my lap in the back seat with Dina.

Dina gave an address to the young man behind the wheel and soon enough we pulled up to someone's house in a residential neighborhood. We left our turkeys with the woman who answered the door.

The next afternoon, two days before Thanksgiving, Woody and Dina went to pick up our dressed birds and returned with two dead, plucked, dressed, and *frozen* turkeys. They'd been frozen solid and stuffed with the feathered heads—with eyes intact—together with the giblets.

Grossed out but undeterred, we set them in the sink overnight to thaw. The next morning we got the heads out and thrown away. I finished off the plucking and gave them a final wash.

Woody made stuffing from the remains of two Pepperidge Farm bags that had exploded in the care-package *en route* from my son Dave in Ohio. I made pumpkin pie from a can and apple pie from scratch. We peeled and sectioned a local pumpkin, simmered the chunks, and called it squash. We boiled some radishes, and we made mashed potatoes and gravy.

The turkeys were delicious. The white meat was moist and the gravy, smooth. With enough butter and salt and pepper, the boiled radishes were even a hit. We intentionally served no bread—standard Kazakh fare—on the principle that two carbohydrates, mashed potatoes and stuffing, are plenty for one meal.

The pies were great. And, when Woody told the story of how the turkey got its name, the locals got a good laugh at the idea that America somehow missed the boat on that one, calling it Turkey.

We ended with our traditional go-around-the-table with everyone saying what they were grateful for. The locals were thankful for the Americans, for the Peace Corps, for learning English, and for the turkey, which they'd never eaten. The Americans were grateful to meet wonderful new friends.

Thanksgiving. Receiving, giving, exchanging, and appreciating: that's what this whole adventure was about, after all.

No one, however, was grateful for the squash.

119

Chapter Twelve
SOME DIFFERENCES WERE HARDER

During our orientation weekend in Washington DC, before our group of 42 had been flown to Almaty, we'd listened to a woman from the Kazakhstan Embassy talk to us about the corruption that enveloped the education system in her country. I'd naively felt that here was where I could make that difference, an easy black and white, an obvious good and bad.

The corruption our speaker had told us about took many forms. It extended from outright extortion—and not one-sided, I'd read, as both teachers and students could be victims—to what could easily be construed as cheating, with the stronger "helping" the weaker.

Fortunately, the extortion examples never crossed my path. My teachers, as I came to call my English teacher colleagues, did not go that route.

And I came to understand that "cheating" could be rather broadly defined. It might even be funny, as I found when I was asked to serve on "the jury" for my college's multi-lingual competition in English, Kazakh, and Russian. I accepted with delight and enormous naiveté.

I walked into the school's auditorium on the second floor, actually a wide expanse in the hallway just as you came out of the stairwell. Large banners hung on the sky-blue curtain that covered the far wall, reminding us in three languages that this competition would determine *The Leader of the 21st Century*. I chuckled inwardly at the idea, but said nothing.

The room was filled with students on folded portable seats bolted together in sets of three. I sat in the front row between two other judges, Gulzhahan to my left and another of the director's assistants—the third of four I'd met—Gulnaz, on my right.

Gulnaz was a bubbly, heavyset woman with bright red lipstick, dark wavy hair, and a complexion that glowed. She knew no English except "I love you," which she proclaimed enthusiastically, along with a bear hug, whenever she saw me.

Each of us had three paddles, the size and shape of ping-pong paddles, made from construction paper and cardboard. At the end of each round, we judges held up our individual ping-pong paddle score, as in the Olympics: 5, 4, or 3, with 5 being the equivalent of an A. There would be no 2s or 1s. Gulnaz took notes.

It was a simple enough setup. A panel of four students sat facing the audience. Off to my right, angled so all could see, two other students took turns reading sets of four questions. Each student got a minute or two to answer each of the questions in a set and, once all four had been answered, we on the jury would raise our paddles with our score.

There were no established criteria for judging an answer, but as the contest progressed and two of the participants had yet to answer one question correctly, it became clear that the sole male student, Azamat, and a young woman named Bota, were in the running to win.

Once, when Azamat sat obviously stumped by a question, Gulzhahan called out the answer to him, in Kazakh.

I poked her. "Hey, you're on the jury," I said, trying to mute my outrage with simple surprise. "You can't give him the answers."

She replied with a hearty laugh. "But he is a good student."

I just looked at her, flummoxed, and heard Azamat give the answer.

We judges did not discuss our scores as we gave them. But once, Gulnaz called out what she wanted mine to be.

"*Pyet*," (five) she told me, "*pye*t."

I ignored her and held up a 3 for Azamat as Gulzhahan and Gulnaz held up their 5s.

"*Pyet, pye*t!" Gulnaz yelled to me, pushing on the paddle I was to use.

I turned to her and said, in English, rather crisply, "But he did not answer one question correctly in this round, not one." I simply couldn't wrap my mind around what was going on here. Why were they letting him skate by? Why were they ignoring Bota, obviously the stronger of the two? *The injustice of it all!*

I stared at Gulnaz and held my #3 paddle for Azamat with pride. Gulnaz stopped yelling in my ear and mysteriously switched her score for Azamat to a 4. From that point on, Azamat never again got another 5 from her, even when he deserved one. *Baffling!*

When the contest was over, according to Gulnaz's notes, which she proudly showed me, there was one point separating Bota from Azamat. Still, Bota was the newly declared *Leader of the 21st Century*. I was proud I could help.

What it would take me months to understand is that what I saw as cheating was actually a show of "collaboration" that I'd simply never encountered before. Since I'd grown up and been educated in a very individualistic culture, I needed to better appreciate the many different ways there are for cultures to function. "Communal," for me, would no longer apply just to hippies living on farms.

My efforts to fit in and better appreciate the culture extended to the friendships I was forging. My Kazakh colleagues laughed easily and often, and that usually endeared them to me. But they also often laughed when the topic was serious, which sometimes disturbed me.

At first, I chalked up what I thought was inappropriate laughter to nervous tension. But one afternoon, while Gulzhahan and I walked along Mira Street, she shared with me a bit of her history that was so poignant that, when she laughed, I understood.

She was explaining to me how difficult the years following independence had been. With the collapse of the Soviet Union in December 1991, Kazakhstan's economic infrastructure fell apart. Commerce as they'd known it came to a halt, and tens of thousands of people were suddenly out of work. The lucky ones who kept their jobs often got no salary. Deliveries of food, even money, stopped.

"You can't imagine how terrible it was," Gulzhahan said.

She told me also of the unusual cold snap that hit during the winter of '93 to '94, when there was neither coal nor fuel oil to run the large central furnaces. She laughed as she told me about this most difficult time of her life. And I could see how laughter helped her process her grief and trauma. Sometimes an event is so absurdly sad that it merits something beyond tears. And what else is there beyond tears but laughter? At least after enough time.

She was right, of course. I couldn't imagine what that time was like, coming as I did from a country that even in our Great Depression of the 1930s, provided a way out for its citizens with the many New Deal programs of President Franklin Delano Roosevelt. But I could try.

I could wrap my mind around how the transition from the Soviet-led, planned economy to sudden independence and a market economy was also a transition from a state-sponsored safety net, which so many took for granted to a new era of personal responsibility that few understood. I'd written my master's thesis on the concept of personal responsibility, specifically on the factors that we humans use in determining whether someone is "able to respond" in a given situation.

As I listened to Gulzhahan's explanation of the personal difficulties of independence, I put my education together with my experience. My Kazakh colleagues believed they had no power, no personal efficacy, no sense of what they could achieve. How could they? They'd never had a chance, so why not just laugh? My role was not to join in their strange laughter but, instead, to simply accept them as they were, as they accepted what they believed to be their fate. As they accepted me for who I was with all the idiosyncrasies and criticism I'd brought with me.

With understanding came compassion. I now understood the earlier comment that had so enflamed me: "Things here will never change." I might hope she was wrong, but at least I no longer felt frustrated by that belief.

Chapter Thirteen
WINTER 2005

After nine months of host family living, we were allowed to move into our own apartment. Gulzhahan found us a first-floor apartment across the playground from Dina's building.

We'd miss watching the sun rise over the reservoir, but we'd stay close to the places that had become part of our world: the *Akimat* (city hall); Company Plus, the Internet cafe; Samadhi, the food store Woody frequented; and the small shop where I had my class handouts copied, whose name I never did figure out.

We hired three of Dina's students to help us move our recent acquisitions: a bookshelf, a small dresser, and a four-inch thick horsehair mattress. We'd had the special mattress made soon after we'd settled in at Dina's, finding that the vertical wooden sideboards, which ran down the center of the bed, interfered with horizontal romantic interludes. The mattress had helped at Dina's, and since we would still have the two-cots-with-sideboards-pushed-together setup, we were hoping we'd have even more call for such cushioning with the added privacy of our very own place.

Our very own place. How I loved the sound of it. As gracious, hospitable, and helpful as Dina had been, we very much needed to be on our own. And, since my meltdown, Woody didn't seem as irritating to me as he had before.

When I accepted that Woody's approach to cross-cultural adjustment was different from mine and made space for his struggles, I stopped judging him so much. Moving forward together once again, we were eager to plan our own meals and have our own guests.

Our new apartment had a similar layout to Dina's, though slightly smaller, and the bedroom and living room were reversed. It was on the first floor, with security bars on the windows and a Peace Corps-mandated metal front door with a peephole.

A half-sized refrigerator, one that might fit under a kitchen counter, was in the bedroom when we first toured the apartment. It hummed incessantly, and our accommodating landlady, Mrs. Kim—she'd married a local Korean man—carted it away and we bought a new one and put it in the kitchen.

Once we'd moved the table for four into the living room and its matching bench for two into the hall, our new refrigerator fit neatly opposite the range, with our electric distiller perched on top. Along the wall between the refrigerator and range, the kitchen window opened out onto a row of large-trunked, lopped-off trees, with the playground beyond. A good view.

Our living room had a green brocade sofa and two overstuffed chairs with a small round table between them. Opposite this sofa, a particleboard bookshelf filled the wall.

I loved our apartment and we felt quickly at home. Our only problem was the bathtub. It was a disgusting shade of "old" with cracks and stains, not something to invite the relaxing soaks I cherished. Gulzhahan volunteered Darkhan to recoat it for us.

I'd had an old tub recoated once before. In Philadelphia, I'd hired a crew who came with an airless paint sprayer and layers of protective material, taped the edges, and completed the job in a few hours. Darkhan arrived with a paintbrush, no protective covering or tape, and spent less than an hour on the project. But when he was done, the tub looked brand new.

The Linens 'N Things shower curtain and coordinating rug that my mother sent were the finishing touches. If I filled the tub and poured in some bubble bath to hide the grayish hue of the water, I could take a hot bath in a tastefully decorated bathroom. I appreciated that not many Peace Corps volunteers get to say this.

❈

One of the best things about being on our own was that we could shop for our own food. Woody prized the local bread, which was still warm if we went out early enough to one of the kiosks along the sidewalks. A loaf of often still-warm bread cost 29 *tenge,* less than a nickel. The price was higher at the food stores, but the selection was greater. Blacks, browns, sourdough, even baguettes were available in addition to three or four types of white, all freshly made, and all local.

Woody liked to shop at Samadhi, a small but well-stocked grocery store across Alashakhana Street. Except for the cream cheese that came in jars, the eggs that came in batches of ten, and the Russian type on the packaging, the Samadhi shelves looked like any shelf in a smallish food store in the States.

I preferred to shop at the Sharwa bazaar. The day we moved to our new apartment, we walked the few blocks to the bazaar in preparation for our first home-cooked meal.

Entering through the well-lit, cavernous produce section full of fresh fruits, nuts, and candies under a sky-blue canopy, we looked over the vegetable section.

"No wonder we never have vegetables," I said to Woody. The pickings were limited to root vegetables. There was lots of cabbage, some of them larger than a basketball. And carrots and potatoes were plentiful. There was a small display of tomatoes and cucumbers, but they looked old. And the only greens we saw were parsley, dill, and sorrel, a lettuce that bore a remarkable resemblance to sour grass. All had been trucked in from Uzbekistan. Nothing was grown in Kazakhstan. And no one seemed to know why.

We wandered past the full array of grains and pastas lining the wall to our left just beyond the main produce aisle, as three women offering identical products sparred over which one would give us the lowest price.

I smiled and gave them a *"Nyet, s'paceba; ne hachoo,"* hoping I was telling them "No thank you; I don't want any," and wishing only that I could say it a bit more gently. Woody seemed not to hear them.

Up four steps from produce and grains, we walked through a door and into a room just for us. Here were the pickles and the bacon Woody coveted and the best *smetana* (sour cream) I'd ever tasted: thick, packed with flavor, and sold freshly ladled into plastic bags. Of course it was delicious; it was 12 percent fat, a fact I gleaned only after I'd become hooked on freshly baked bread with a thick layer of *smetana*, the perfect accompaniment to a cup of *chai* with jam.

Woody hovered over a deli-like case that held Korean salads, while I took note of the freezer case containing, among many things I didn't recognize, one that I did: frozen pizza dough. We stocked up on bacon, pickles, and *smetana* before heading to the room with the meat.

It was all unpackaged and fresh, the slaughtering done in a small anteroom. I recognized the beef section by the severed cow's head that gazed up at the ceiling from the corner of a table. The sheep's head on the corner of another table advertised the mutton section, as did the pig's head for the pork. Though Muslims took their pork prohibition seriously—more so than their alcohol prohibition—the Russian Orthodox believers had no such restriction, and pork was plentiful.

Chickens, though, were nowhere to be found at the Sharwa Bazaar. If we wanted chicken, we'd need to go to a store like

Samadhi or Dana. There, we'd find double joints piled high in the freezer case, unwrapped and ready to go.

Back in our apartment, we unloaded our treasures. I made us each a cup of tea and we sat at our table across from one another in our tiny living room.

"Here we are," I said to Woody. He smiled as he leaned forward to add sugar to his tea.

"Yes, here we are. Home at last," and we clinked our teacups together in a toast to our new home.

It had been a long road to get where we were now. We weren't yet halfway through this Peace Corps journey, but I believed we could handle whatever lay ahead. At least now we'd have a place to retreat to.

Home had been what I'd given up to go on this adventure. And we were, slowly, crafting ourselves a new one, however different it was from what I'd had back in the States. I closed my eyes and sighed deeply with satisfaction.

⊱※⊰

Now settled in our new apartment, we were free to hold social activities as often as we wished, and we wished to often. Our first gathering was with my "movie night advisory committee."

Every Peace Corps volunteer has not only the job they are assigned to, but also a "community project" that they devise themselves, some activity that involves the wider community.

I'd had my heart set on showing American movies since I first heard of this requirement. My plan was to introduce American culture to students and the public through weekly movies. Each movie would meet one of three criteria: it would portray a real person from American history, a real time in American history, or real scenes from the American landscape. And I'd put out the word to my friends and family in the States to send me DVDs that they loved and which fit the criteria.

131

My biggest concern about showing films was that my audience, accustomed to watching the shoot-'em-ups and chase-'em-downs that sold all over town, wouldn't be willing to sit through two hours of dialogue and character development. So I decided on an advisory committee of locals, a cultural insurance policy of sorts, to help me decide which films would be the most compelling for my intended audience.

Gulzhahan, Dina, and redheaded Natasha, Woody's new counterpart (his original counterpart, Aniya, had disappeared, something unfortunately too common among Peace Corps counterparts) joined three other women I was eager to get to know better, Aigul, Yulia, and Togzhan, a friend of one of Dina's sisters.

My committee of six agreed to monthly Sunday afternoon meetings at our place. Woody would have his own community project, but I included him in each of our meetings and he eagerly participated.

On the third Sunday afternoon in January, four of my six gathered in our apartment at about 3 pm. I welcomed the women into my home and, over tea and apple pie, told them what I had in mind.

"I'd like you to preview each movie on my laptop. To watch it here on a Sunday afternoon." They nodded in approval. "I want to make sure it's a movie that is right for the town."

It was their "thumbs up" I was seeking. They seemed to understand, though I believe the idea of turning a "thumbs down" never entered their minds.

"And I want you to get your students to come. And your colleagues."

"That will be hard," Dina offered. "The teachers have to work, then make dinner. It's very hard to get our teachers out at night."

Indeed. I'd heard this before. The teachers who had families were busy. They were tired. And going to an English-language movie was not going to be a priority for them. Still, to a person, each woman left telling me her students would come. She'd make sure of it.

I was satisfied. I'd thrown my first social function in our new place, and I felt encouraged that my movie night project was going to be a success. I wondered, however, if our meetings served more as a means for them to practice their English than to make my community project work.

Long before opening night, I put together a vocabulary list for our first movie, *Sleepless in Seattle*. Yulia translated it into Russian and Togzhan made sufficient copies to hand out. But one week before we were to show the film, it still hadn't come in the mail. The chance of it arriving in time was getting too slim.

I called a special meeting of the advisory committee and, gathered in my living room, they solved our first crisis, quickly choosing *Forrest Gump* from the eighteen movies I already had on hand. I found an extensive vocabulary list for it at ESLNotes.com that needed only a little editing to eliminate the Australian twang.

Yulia translated again and Togzhan made more copies. Disaster was averted. What I had dubbed "Monday Night is English Movie Night in Zhezkazgan. Pass it on," would open as planned.

My new home was now home base to my developing relationships with a group of smart women. If my community project served a dual purpose for them in giving them a chance to practice their English, it would serve a dual purpose for me as well, a chance to feel the special bond of female companionship once again.

I was feeling fully settled in Zhezkazgan by the time the first movie night arrived. I'd gotten through my first big bout of culture shock, though there would surely be more to come, and I was back on familiar ground with Woody.

On the first Monday in February, Saryarka, the local theater, which seated 150 people in six-to-a-table restaurant style, was practically full. I stood up from my table to make my way to the front of the room, excited.

Speaking one sentence at a time so that Gulzhahan (in Kazakh) and Aigul (in Russian) could read their transcriptions, I introduced myself, thanked the necessary people, and gave a little speech.

> *I love movies for many different reasons. Movies transport us to places too far for us to travel, to times that are past, and to times that haven't yet come. Movies introduce us to new people: people we like, understand, and love; and people we don't like, can't understand, and maybe even fear.*

As my translators spoke, I looked out into the audience. Woody, at our table as close to the front as the seating would allow, gave me a smile. I believed he felt as excited at my premier as I did.

My translators and I carried on.

> *Good movies show us truths about human nature, truths that exist beyond culture and national boundaries. Good movies can challenge our way of looking at the world. There are movies that help us better understand why we see the world as we do. And, perhaps most importantly, there are movies that help us understand why others see the world differently. The movies I have collected will, I hope, expose you to particular regions of America, particular periods of its history, or particular real life Americans with important stories to tell.*

I paused again to take in the scene. The theater was dark, with only a few stage lights in front and the lights from the projection room up high at the back. And in that darkness I was standing, speaking before more than one hundred people and hadn't thought once of my stuttering. I felt only the exhilaration of my project taking hold and flying.

"Through these movies," I continued, "I hope you will come to understand, enjoy, and appreciate the America I love. Through these movies, I also hope you will begin to find English a little easier to understand."

I ended with details of how *Monday Night at the Movies* would work: same movie throughout the month, free vocabulary handouts. I thanked Rasia, the theater manager, for reducing the ticket price, and introduced the movie.

Forrest Gump made a perfect opening movie, displaying both the magnificent American landscape and recent American history with a fairy-tale quality I'd forgotten about. It was well received, and I got a few thumbs-ups from the students as they filed out. But the best acknowledgment came from Timur, a tall university student whom we'd get to know better during our second year. He shook my hand as Dina, Woody, and I were getting into our taxi, and addressed me in heavily accented English.

"Thank you for doing this. This is exactly what our town needs."

Just what the town needed! That was a high compliment indeed. As I climbed into bed that night the words of the post office woman who had berated me months earlier rang in my head.

"You're in Kazakhstan now!" she had screamed.

Yes, I was. And I was fine with that. I rolled over, put my arm around Woody's middle, and drifted off to sleep.

❦

My advisory committee continued to meet monthly on Sunday afternoons at our home, although no more than four of the seven members ever showed up at one time. It was indeed a way for them to practice their English, but it quickly became a way for me to practice my understanding of cultural quirks.

One Sunday afternoon, Gulzhahan, Togzhan, and Yulia arrived and we started our meeting off with *chai* and a chocolate pudding cake I'd made. Socializing always came before business, and I was letting myself learn to enjoy this in spite of the fact that my inner taskmaster felt a bit neglected. As we were about to start the meeting, Dina arrived, explaining that her sister had been visiting.

"Would you like some tea?" I asked her automatically.

"No, thank you," she replied, also automatically, as she took off her coat. Then I remembered: one doesn't ask in Kazakhstan, one simply serves.

"You take sugar and milk, yes?" I offered, catching my mistake.

"Yes, thank you," she said as she removed her shoes.

I not only poured her tea, I cut her a piece of chocolate pudding cake. She didn't eat it, but that was not the point. The piece was hers, whether she wanted it or not. I was catching on.

I arrived at the teachers' lounge early one morning in mid-February to find most of my colleagues gathered around the table involved in serious conversation, but with no *chai*.

Always, when there were so many teachers together, there would be *chai*. But this day there was only the group of teachers sitting together grumbling to each other, also unusual for those normally so accepting.

"What's going on?" I inquired of no one in particular.

"We haven't gotten our salaries," Assem responded.

"We won't get paid," Tolganay added at the same time. "Again."

"I don't understand. What happened? Why aren't you getting paid?"

"We don't know. Teachers in the schools just got their salary for December. We thought we'd get ours, too. But they say, 'next week.'"

"Who says?"

"Our bookkeeper."

Noses curled at the mention of the college's bookkeeper. I was baffled, but by now I knew that further questions would not necessarily bring me further enlightenment.

Later, sitting in the café, the grumbling continued across three tables. Gulzhahan explained the situation to me and, as usual when she spoke, everyone else became still.

"We've been told 'next week' since before New Year's. I think our bookkeeper doesn't send the papers on time."

I couldn't help but think of the story of the spider and the fly. After we got our *chai* and a pastry, I decided to tell the story.

"Do you know the story of the spider and the fly?" I asked and all heads shook. "Well, there is this spider, you see. She's built herself a beautiful web and one day a fly is caught in it. The fly says to the spider, 'Oh please, pretty spider. Set me free. I must get home to my family.' The spider looks at the fly and says, 'Don't worry. Tomorrow I shall set you free.' The next day comes and again the fly asks, 'Please, spider; won't you let me go? I must get home to my children.' And again the spider says, 'Tomorrow you shall go free.' This goes on for a few days until finally, the fly dies and the spider eats him. The moral of the story: Tomorrow never comes."

Gulzhahan laughed heartily and immediately, as did Assem and Tolganay, who understood my English well enough to follow. Gulzhahan translated for the rest, and laughter followed, the first I'd heard all day.

"Yes, and 'next week' never comes," remarked Assem. "I will remember that."

"Has this happened before?" I asked, wanting to figure it out.

"Yes, this happens every year."

"Why?"

Gulzhahan repeated her theory that the paperwork from the college did not get to the central office in Karaganda in time. But others had different theories. Some said the bookkeeper was lazy, or was stealing the money. Some thought the bookkeeper was not to blame; it was someone at the Ministry of Education at the *Akimat* (city hall).

Theories flew about and my colleagues were at a loss as to what to do. They didn't know where their salaries came from, who set them, or who distributed them. They didn't know whom to blame and, therefore, they didn't know what to do, except complain. I was infuriated on their behalf.

Late pay or partial pay, neither was unusual apparently. Dina had told us she was getting only eighty percent of her salary.

"There are not so many students this year," she'd told us when we still lived with her, "and not so much money to pay."

Rather than reducing the staff, there was an across-the-board reduction in pay, so everyone got less, but everyone continued to work. At least Dina's colleagues agreed on the reason. There were simply not enough students. It was not so simple for Gulzhahan's group.

Though unionism runs in my blood, I was not about to lead a teachers' strike. Not only would the Peace Corps send me home immediately, it was not my place and I knew that. Still, I couldn't resist.

"Do you know what a strike is?" I asked with feigned nonchalance.

"We cannot. We will lose our jobs," was the chorus. They knew the word.

"You won't lose your jobs," I told them, knowing that English teachers were in short supply, and knowing that these teachers, at least most of them, were great at what they did.

"The director says he'll fire us if we don't work." And they believed him.

I didn't know what power the director actually held, and realized that whatever I thought I knew, there was so much more I didn't. So, I backed off.

Chapter Fourteen
MUD SEASON 2005

I walked up the stairs of my college and past the old woman who washed the floors every day. Unruly grey hair stuck out under her headscarf, and gnarled fingers rinsed her filthy rag in a bucket of black water.

Twisting the rag, she placed it back on the end of the two-foot-long broom, and continued her work, dragging her homemade mop across the next step. The water had been dirty since the third step, and she had four more flights of stairs ahead. It was well into March and mud season was here.

During mud season, winter hung around all night, spring showed up in the morning, summer was in full swing by noon, and by dinnertime, it was autumn.

Room 42 faced east, pulling in the sun's heat all morning, while the central heating system, from far outside of town, was pumping steam into the radiators beneath the wall of closed windows as though it were still winter. By eleven o'clock, when I arrived with Tolganay to teach, the room was too hot to sit in, never mind learn in.

"Bulan," I asked the young student in the back of the room, near the window, "please open the window." Bulan didn't move, and I assumed it was because he didn't understand me. "Bulan," I repeated, and this time I added hand gestures to my "please open the window."

"No. I, no. Miss Janet."

Bulan was the only student who called me Miss Janet. He had a broad, quick smile whenever he greeted me in the hall with his, "Hello, Miss Janet," and I'd been initially charmed until I realized it was pretty much all he could say in English.

"We cannot open the window," added one of my front-row students.

These were great windows, a good twelve feet high, covering the outer wall from above the radiators to the ceiling, and I'd often seen them opened during the fall semester, so I knew they could be opened, like very large, very old, doors, even on their creaky side hinges.

"Why can't you open the window?" Even with my best efforts to stop analyzing everything, I hadn't been able to stop asking why, but at least I'd become aware when I did.

"We must pay 1,500 *tenge* to open the window," the student said. I was missing something. Fifteen hundred *tenge* was about ten dollars. It was also a day's salary for some teachers. I turned to Tolganay, my co-teacher for the class.

"It's true," she said. "We must pay 1,500 *tenge* to open the window."

I laughed aloud, a guffaw that surprised and then embarrassed me. *Too loud.* I didn't want to appear rude or, worse, arrogant. But we were trying to teach a class and it was so hot the sweat dripped down onto my glasses. My blouse was already soaked, back and front.

The window functioned properly but someone, somewhere had created a silly rule and everyone felt bound by it. No one, at least no one I'd met, questioned rules.

I stared for a moment at Tolganay, hoping she'd give me some explanation.

"The bookkeeper," she started. "If we want to open the window, the bookkeeper says we must pay 1,500 *tenge* to her."

The same bookkeeper I'd heard was responsible for those missing salaries in February?

"The windows are fragile," she added, anticipating my ever-present *Why?* "They may break."

"If she asks for 1,500 *tenge*. I'll pay it. Let's open the window."

I'd gone along with the school's rules all year, not wanting to impose my way before I'd learned theirs. Now I was ready to push back.

I smiled at Tolganay, waiting for her response.

"I'm afraid," she mumbled, and she stood stiff, unable, it seemed, to move.

I didn't want to jeopardize her job, but I also didn't want to join in their fearful inertia. I didn't want her to suffer, but we could not teach in a sauna.

"I'll take the responsibility," I offered again, seeking in her agreement the permission to do what I wanted to do. All I wanted was a nod. But she stayed still, her eyes wide. So, instead, I took her lack of disagreement as the permission I sought and walked to the back of the room, determined to open the window.

If anyone should break the rule, it should be me. But when I tried to open it and the hinge stuck, I realized I didn't have the strength. *A fine kettle of fish.*

Before I'd thought what I'd do next, Bulan popped up to help me. Together we gently pried it open, letting a refreshing gust of air blow in.

The students sat with their mouths open, literally. They dropped their jaws and gaped at me. *I'd always thought that was just a figure of speech.* Then, as I walked between rows of desks, back to the front, they began to smile, some even laughed. *What had I done?*

I didn't want to condone anarchy. I certainly didn't want to give the impression that I thought I was above the law. By the time I got back to the front, I had an idea.

I wrote "Rule of Law" in big letters on the blackboard.

"Laws are important," I said. "Rules are important. In America, we have a long history of breaking unfair or unjust laws and rules. If rules are not made with input from the people," I preached, "the people don't always follow them."

I began to say something about "civil disobedience," but realized I was long past their level of English understanding. I abandoned my soapbox and we moved into the lesson for the day. Next year, I knew, I would get to teach them about Martin Luther King Jr. I had plenty of time to get my soapbox ready for that.

Before I left the room, I closed the window. I'd learned when to push, but there was no sense in flaunting it. Besides, with the mud drying up, even the slightest breeze through the window left a fine coating of dust everywhere you looked. It was the least I could do.

❧❦❧

"All you Americans ask 'why' all the time." Assem's simple comment caught me by surprise. But it didn't surprise me.

I'd first met Assem in late September, upon her return from a lengthy maternity leave. I was smitten with her shiny black hair and her California-cheerleader spunk, and she quickly became the easiest of my colleagues to talk to. Not only because she wasn't shy, which she wasn't. Her English just seemed to come more naturally. And I soon discovered why.

She'd traveled to England as a 12-year-old shortly after independence, through a government-sponsored exchange program, and spent a few months living with a local family there. That experience had definitely left its mark on her, in both her language skill and her outlook on the wider world.

Woody loved what he called her "radio voice" and I, eventually, loved her laugh. But I hadn't always loved her laugh. In fact, sometime during that second semester Assem was at the center of what was my final "attack"—I can't think of a better word—of frustration.

Thanks to friends in the US, I'd accumulated a collection of VHS films in a format that could be used in Kazakhstan. Gulzhahan had offered her tape player and apartment one Saturday afternoon and invited the four of us over to watch them and help me decide how best to use them in my classroom. Or so I thought.

I'd arrived at the appointed time with a half-dozen videos I thought could offer interesting lessons. But once again, I was the first to arrive. Right on time. While we waited for the others, Gulzhahan put in a video from my Ohio friend Amy. It was an animated history of the hot dog and I was just beginning to see some potential for the classroom when she clicked it off.

"This is not interesting," she said, and searched for another tape.

And so it went, fifteen minutes of one, ten minutes of another, five of a third. It was annoying in the way a husband-with-the-remote can be annoying. I'd just be getting into the story line and CLICK, Gulzhahan would stop it and put in another. My irritation grew, but I said nothing.

When the others arrived, Gulzhahan served lunch. It was 2 pm and I'd eaten lunch before I came. Silly me. Of course there'd be a meal. There was always a meal. There was the requisite laughter during the meal—that too-loud, insistent, irritating laughter that had so bothered me at first.

Sister Act with Whoopi Goldberg was playing in the background but no one was watching. It was clear no one had much interest in watching the American videos I'd so painstakingly chosen. I sat—quiet, patient, and sullen—while the four bantered on in Kazakh. Surely we'd settle down and get serious after the meal was finished? But when Gulzhahan began to clear the dishes, Assem announced that she had to get home, and Gulzhan and Tolganay agreed that the time was indeed getting late.

"What about the movie!" I exclaimed, shocked.

I'd just given three hours of my life to this project and I expected to leave knowing which movies would work for which of my classes. I expected them to take this planning session seriously. I expected them to care. I expected them to work. I expected.

"It's not important," Assem said. "We can watch it another time." And she laughed as she went to retrieve her jacket.

"It's not funny!" I shouted at her, pulling on my own boots. If they were leaving, so was I. "Why did we come here?" I asked, consciously keeping myself from saying what I really wanted to say: "What a colossal waste of time."

Though I'd call many women friends while there, these were the closest, and the most consistently-in-my-life ones I had in Zhezkazgan. I didn't want to hurt their feelings. Still. I thought only of the time that had been wasted.

"We wanted to watch the movie," Gulzhan offered quietly.

"Well, how could we when you all kept talking? We got nothing done. What a waste of time. This was a big waste of time." There, I'd said it. At least I'd not said "colossal."

They had looks of such utter confusion and dismay that I immediately wanted to take back my words. I couldn't remember a time I'd felt so totally frustrated, so angry, so completely out of control, and so very, very tired. I had to get away before I said something else I'd regret.

I swung my arms into my coat, ignoring Gulzhahan's bewilderment, Assem's protests, and Gulzhan and Tolganay's quiet stares, and headed down the six flights of stairs, out into the cold, and home, where I peeled off my coat, climbed onto my bed and sobbed, an utter failure at this "make friends for America" crap.

The fourth-year students didn't begin the second semester until March. Instead, they were scattered throughout the region at village schools for a required two-month teaching practicum.

When they returned, Gulsana, one of my favorite students from English 49, asked me to meet her in the café. I loved being her teacher. She was a student any teacher would enjoy: eager, curious, and responsible. I could always count on her to "get it."

We sat across from each other at a table in the back corner. She was thinner and more subdued than she'd been during the fall semester. And she seemed hesitant to speak. I was concerned for her.

"What's up?" I asked, experimenting with a new idiom. To my delight, she knew it.

After a few rounds of small talk, she got serious. "I've met someone. Janet, I'm in love."

She sounded scared, sad maybe.

"He's a policeman in Satpaev. He's from the south. I cannot tell my mother. What should I do?"

Were she American, I'd have been on familiar ground. I'd have told her to lighten up, enjoy being in love, but not to make any life-changing decisions like getting married.

Being in love is wonderful fun, but, as Woody claimed when we first fell in love, it's also madness. Ours had been a glorious madness and I fully enjoyed it at the time. We'd both enjoyed our love even more when it became more serene, more adult, saner. Slower; it took us three years after I moved to Philly before we lived together, and another two years before we married.

Gulsana was still in her madness. If she were Scandinavian, Australian, even Dutch, I'd have known what to tell her. But for a Kazakh, I was stumped. I wasn't sure what the cultural implications were for this love she'd fallen into. I did, however, understand her reluctance to tell her mother.

Gulsana's mother had reason to worry. Or would, at least, think she did. The Kazakhstan of ancient times, known more precisely as the Kazakh Khanate, or land ruled by a Kazakh Khan (King), had been divided into three regions (*zhuze*) with vastly different priorities and abilities and each ruled by their own Khan. The Little *Zhuze*, in the north, had been the land of the farmers. The Great *Zhuze*, in the south, where Gulsana's boyfriend was from, had been the land of the warriors, the fighters. And in the center, the steppe, the Middle *Zhuze*, where we were, had been the land of the academics.

The three Kazakh *zhuze*s had been separate and distinct for 600 years, since the death of Genghis Khan. And their absorption into Russia's shadow came slowly, as the khan of each *zhuze* turned (independently from each other) to the Russian monarchy for protection from invading tribes from the east. Russia was happy to provide protection, ousting the invading Jungars, and, within 150 years, controlling what is now Central Asia.

History like this might not matter in today's American society, though there are always elements in any culture that set limits on whom one should marry, but history matters a great deal in Kazakhstan. For a daughter from either the Middle or the Lesser *Zhuze* to marry a man from the Great *Zhuze* would be worrisome for a mother from a culture where such distinctions still mattered, like the modern and now-united Kazakhstan. Indeed, the southern region, from Almaty west to the lower Caspian Sea, boasted a growing religious fundamentalism not seen further north. Simply put, women didn't fare as well in the south of Kazakhstan as they might in the other regions.

Gulsana wanted me to tell her what to do. Since I didn't know, I would err on the side of caution.

"You need to talk to your mother," I repeated.

She insisted that she could not. She was smitten and she was scared. So what more could I say? I could only listen, and I did. Through a second cup of *chai*.

I entertained a fleeting "if only" when we finally parted. *If only she were going to the States this summer.*

Early in the fall semester, Gulsana had come to class more excited than usual.

"I have $3,000 and I want to go to America," she'd exclaimed. "What shall I do? Where shall I go?"

I'd had no idea. But now I wished I'd followed through on finding out. *If only I had a way to give her a break from her predicament and a chance at foreign travel all at once.*

Gulsana's situation haunted me, and motivated me to find a way for my students and maybe even my colleagues to see America. And if that couldn't happen for whatever reason, surely there was a way for them to see some of the rest of the world—the Netherlands, for example, where everyone spoke English, or India, Scandinavia, even England. Travel opened a person up and changed him or her.

I wanted my students and colleagues to know what the renowned cellist Yo-Yo Ma knew. "When we enlarge our view of the world," he once said, "we deepen our understanding of our own lives." The Peace Corps was giving me that deepening view, and I wanted no less for them.

Gulsana gave me the necessary motivation, but it would take me most of the following year to figure out how to make it happen.

Before I could focus on helping anyone experience world travel, however, I had to get my fourth-year students back to a routine. This was easier said than done.

Gulsana was now often absent, as were many of the returning fourth-year students. One Friday, only seven showed up for my optional English 49 class that usually had twenty-six. With such a small group, it was time to try something new.

We moved chairs into a small circle in the front of the room and I sat quietly, waiting for the students to take the initiative.

It's an old Gestalt therapist trick, curious to see where the conversation would go if I didn't lead it. Who, or even what, might arise if I just sat back? Do all groups need a leader?

Gulya, who normally sat in the second row behind Gulsana's empty seat, began immediately.

"Our books are bad, there is no quality, and the TV shows are poor. How can we feel patriotic if there is nothing to be proud of?"

I hadn't seen this coming. *Where had she done her practice teaching?*

"Everyone knows we have no textbooks," she continued.

"We do have textbooks!" the others chorused in determined opposition.

"We could have more," Dinara added more quietly, "but we do have them."

The others nodded.

"They are bad. They are filled with mistakes. They are old. They are worse than nothing." *Had Gulya been reading my journal?*

Though I agreed with her, I wasn't about to admit it. I was more interested in the process unfolding before me, a debate that never once veered out of English.

Gulya was the first local person I'd met in my now seven months of living in Zhezkazgan who spoke aloud about the problems that had initially frustrated me.

"We love our life here," offered Dinara.

"Can you use 'I' and say that again?" I finally snuck in, wanting to encourage each student to speak only for him or herself.

"I love my life here," she said, smiling in recognition of the difference.

The rest were eager to agree with Dinara, who continued. "Yes, we have a good life. We have many architectural artifacts," she continued.

I was gathering from the spontaneous debate before me that to have complaints about your country appeared to be unpatriotic. This interested me. And, whereas only a few weeks earlier I would have thrust my own opinion on my students—that to question the government can be an act of patriotism—now I just tried to listen and understand.

"We do not," countered Gulya. "I have been to Bulgaria. They have many. We have very few." I stifled a smile.

As proud as I was of myself for letting everyone's opinions unfold without my interference, I was also proud of Gulya. It was unusual for someone to stand apart from the group on any topic, in any country, never mind one as communally focused as Kazakhstan, and she was doing so with gusto. But when the class left for the day, I watched as she walked out alone.

In our apartment, our quirky oven was beyond help. Darkhan, Gulzhahan's husband, had been over several times to fix it, rewiring something each time, helping it limp along. But the quirkiness had lost its appeal, and I finally bought a new one.

As with all the stoves I'd seen, it was white, narrow, and had just three burners. But at least they all worked when turned on. The back left quadrant of the stove, where a burner would be at home, had a place for a hot dish, a good thing since our kitchen provided no other surface for hot things.

Mr. Kim carted the old one off to join our original refrigerator and TV, storing them until we moved out.

We paid a reasonable 31,000 *tenge* (about $170) for the stove, delivered. But when the men from the store set it up, they couldn't plug it in. The oven plug had three prongs and our wall outlet, two.

"I want to call an electrician," I told Gulzhahan when I telephoned her. "Who do I call?" There were no Yellow Pages in Zhezkazgan, but *surely the town would have professional electricians.* I was prepared to pay whatever it cost.

"Darkhan is better," Gulzhahan insisted.

They came to the apartment the next day. Darkhan, equipped with just a single screwdriver and quick smile, was smart and reliable and a pleasure to have around.

He'd call out his customary "Hallo, how are you?" as he entered, with equal emphasis on each word, the extent of his English. I was sure Gulzhahan prompted him on the walk over.

Gulzhahan and I had *chai* while Darkhan replaced the wall outlet. I had no trouble with him trying to get our old oven to work, and I certainly appreciated his being available to get our new one plugged in. I only wondered if we were taking advantage of them. This was beyond what a counterpart should be doing. But it was, I realized happily, what a friend would do.

I found another friend that spring when Gulzhahan decided Gulzhan, one of the English teachers, would become my new "Russian tutor."

Our tutoring sessions were simple walks through town over lunch, where we'd have *samsas* (fried meat or cheese-filled pastries) and talk. She'd prompt me on what to say and I'd do the ordering at the take-out window.

"*Dva s'surom, pajalsta*" (two with cheese, please) and we'd roost somewhere close by to eat them.

Gulzhan was easy to talk to, especially once we switched to English. I was a terribly unmotivated Russian student and she was an eager-to-improve English teacher, so our sessions always devolved into English, with a smattering enough of Russian so she wouldn't balk when I paid her the 200 *tenge* that the Peace Corps would reimburse me. She was about my height and, as we walked along Zhezkazgan's sidewalks, conversation came easily.

Gulzhan's mother had been an active and dedicated Communist. When the Soviet Union dissolved in 1991 and the

Communist Party lost favor, her mother's life as she'd known it ended, and she was dead of cancer within two years. Gulzhan's sadness as she told me the story was clear.

Until these talks, I'd not given much thought to how deeply the Soviet mindset, the Communist mindset, had taken hold among the local Kazakh population. Of course, membership in the Communist Party was voluntary, but during Soviet times, one did not advance at work, at least in the cities, if one was not a member. Then, with the flick of a pen, the dogma that had ruled their lives, their parents' lives, and their grandparents' lives was gone.

My struggles with cultural adjustment paled! Through Gulzhan and my other colleagues, I realized that I was not alone in needing to deal with adapting to new and strange ways. They'd also had to do it, had been doing it, for the past fifteen years.

Chapter Fifteen
SPRING 2005

Spring, officially beginning on March 1, couldn't come soon enough for me, and with it came Nauryz (pronounced NOW ruz), a holiday celebrated on March 22. Observed throughout Central Asia and beyond, it is perhaps the oldest holiday in recorded history, a contribution originally from the ancient Persian religion, Zoroastrianism. It's New Year's Day for the nearly one and a half billion Muslims around the world, and I had never heard of it.

Banned during Soviet times, Nauryz still wasn't an official holiday in Kazakhstan, but schools, banks, and businesses across the nation closed. The entire town, it seemed, flowed down Alashakhana, despite the fact that the day was cold and cloudy with a raw wind that made being outside most unpleasant.

Food vendors lined one side of the street, selling their deep-fried *samsas* and freshly grilled *shashlik*. Soft drinks and pastries covered their tables, and I saw blue cotton candy sold in plastic bags. Now this was a holiday! Softly rounded, felt-covered yurts, collapsible circular tents, reminders of a long-ago life, filled the other side of the broad avenue.

Each yurt belonged to a local organization and was open to the public, many serving a meal inside. I walked through one where the layout reflected tradition. The door faced south; the "men's area" (where weapons for hunting and other implements hung on the wall) was to the west; the "women's area" (the kitchen) faced east.

In ancient times, the head of the house would sit facing the door. In the center would be a small fire and above it, open to the sky and allowing smoke from the fire to escape, a *shanyrak* (center wheel), as important a symbol of the Kazakh home as our hearth or our kitchen table is for Americans.

Woody and I continued up Alashakhana to Mira. Both were wide avenues and, since they were closed to traffic for the Nauryz celebration, the intersection was the perfect place to offer pony rides, Kazakh style. I watched as one young girl climbed on for her ride, sitting in front of the handler, who kicked the horse into a fast gallop and through the crowded street. People jumped out of the way, missed by inches.

Insurance regulations? Obviously none.

Nauryz is a happy holiday, the symbolic start of a new year. Nauryz also ushers in the "new year" in relationships. Debts are paid and family members or neighbors who have fought during the year, reconcile.

For me, Nauryz was the symbol of a new commitment to my students and my colleagues. I would be going to Almaty in a few weeks for a conference, and while there I wanted to make good on my intention to find the venues through which my Kazakh students or colleagues could travel abroad.

After hearing too many students inform me, in earnest, that Kazakhstan was a "world leader," I wanted to expose them to the wider world. Living in another culture changes and challenges a person, and I wanted my students to have that experience. I was determined to find ways to guide them into it, at least those who wanted such an experience.

April arrived, and Gulzhahan and I were finally off to Almaty and the annual teacher's conference I'd been anticipating: the National Association of Teachers of English in Kazakhstan, or NATEK.

We took the train to Almaty, where the Peace Corps housed us, with the other grant recipients and volunteers, at a hotel near the American Embassy: five Peace Corps volunteers on the first floor and Gulzhahan and eleven other local teachers upstairs.

The Peace Corps had sponsored five volunteers—those who were presenting papers—to come to the conference. I'd written my paper initially as an article entitled *How My Gestalt Training Informs My Teaching*. I'd re-titled it as *The Courage to Speak* when I submitted it for the conference, but it had mysteriously morphed to *Getting Shy Students to Speak* by the time I found it in the program.

Gulzhahan suggested I give a preview of my talk to the group of local counterparts, a typically good idea from her. But these village teachers did not understand enough English to follow a presented paper. So, after they settled onto two large sofas and a few club chairs around a large coffee table, I began with an exercise.

"As you sit there," I said to them, "fold your hands, like this." I showed them my hands, folded as though I were going to twiddle my thumbs. "Go ahead," I encouraged them, "do it now."

They did, and I continued. "Notice where your thumbs are. Some of you will have the left thumb on top, some the right. It doesn't matter where your thumbs are, just notice."

I saw them comparing their hands with each other and heard the background hum getting louder. They wanted to know what was going on, which way was the correct way. Gulzhahan translated quietly.

"Now, open your fingers."

I showed them what I meant by unraveling my own hands and reversing the natural way my fingers entangled with one another.

"Move your fingers so the opposite thumb is on top, with the rest of the fingers following."

They followed, though tentatively.

"Now sit quietly and notice your hands." I gave them a few moments. "How does it feel? What do you want to do?"

Again, Gulzhahan translated.

Mumblings of, "It's uncomfortable. I want to put my fingers back," broke through the foreign words. It was just what I'd hoped for. I was ready to make my point, a lesson for me to remember as well.

"When things are uncomfortable," I began, "we all want to go back to the comfortable, the familiar. But, sometimes it's important not to go back. We have a choice. If we can let ourselves be uncomfortable for a bit, we can learn new ways."

I knew it would be hard for Kazakh teachers to change. Heck, it's hard for anyone. The real problem was, I thought, that perhaps some didn't really want to.

The old Soviet ways, based in fear and humiliation, made me shudder. I'd heard teachers complain about their "lazy" students who sat in the back of the room and never participated. I knew too many teachers either ignored them or screamed at them, earnestly believing in some direct relationship between the amount of humiliation they could exact and the student's ability to learn.

I wanted them to consider, at least, that another way might be possible.

"It's a choice we have, to try what is uncomfortable," I told them, their fingers still obediently folded in front of them. I hoped they'd understand the value in trying something new. "It will be worth it for your students. And for you."

The women listened politely, but there were no questions, no conversation after, no feedback at all. If I were in an

American lecture hall, I'd be embarrassed by the silence. But I was in Kazakhstan, where any professed "expert" was listened to with respect and never, ever questioned. And my metaphorical fingers intertwined uncomfortably.

❦

Gulzhahan took the train back to Zhezkazgan alone, while I kept an appointment at the American Embassy, eager to learn about programs to help my students get to America. But first I'd spend the intervening two days with my former host mother, Hadija, in nearby Esik. I couldn't wait.

When my taxi dropped me off at the gate in front of her house, I could barely contain my excitement in seeing her again. The first time we'd met, at the beginning of our training, we'd hugged instinctively. Hadija had an earth-mother air about her that had made me feel, in that moment of complete unknowing, safe in her hands.

She must have heard the taxi for there she was right away, wiping her hands on her apron, smiling that wide, gold-toothed grin, and opening her arms to embrace me once again. She was also my friend.

"*Drast v'witchya. Kak dila,*" I said, giving my standard, automatic Russian "Hello. How are you?" and grateful I remembered since Hadija spoke no English. She also spoke no Kazakh.

"*Drast v'witchya. Kharashow. Ochin kharashow, seechas,*" (Hello. Good. Very good, now) she proclaimed in her clear, slow voice that was so easy for me to follow. Then she yelled for her children to come.

Takhmina and Fatima, the older two, came with warm Russian greetings as well. Soniya, my English-speaking savior in all things language-related, and Murcel, the youngest, were still in school.

159

"*Dobra pahzhalh vaht, Tetchka Dzhanet,*" (Welcome, Aunt Janet) Fatima said to me, with her gentle almost shy smile.

She wasn't shy, I knew that already. Demure just seemed to be her way in the world. Takhmina, the more exuberant middle daughter, giggled and gave me a hug.

Hadija had taken my suitcase from the driver, chatted with him as though they were old friends, and was going into the house with it by the time my hellos were done. I followed her, grateful to be once again cocooned within this strong, loving family. My visit, only two nights, would be too short.

The first night we watched a video I'd brought, *Miracle on Ice*, the story of the 1980 Olympic hockey game between Russia and America. It was in English and I'd brought it with Soniya in mind, but her brother and father quickly joined us. Hadija, Fatima, and Takhmina were bustling in the kitchen uninterested.

Suddenly, Hadija came into the living room and began talking to her husband, Mamluk. I had no idea what she was saying. She talked faster when she wasn't talking to me. Besides, I was engrossed in the movie.

"Shhhh," I hissed to her, with a smile. "I can't hear."

And as the words came out I realized I was not a guest in this home. I was family. And I liked it much better than being a "gift from God."

Mamluk was a strong yet quiet man, about my age. He worked as a long-distance truck driver, taking milk either to or from—I never could figure that part out—Uzbekistan to the south. But he had a ready wit about him and when I teased him by calling him "Papaluk," he understood the joke and always laughed.

On the second and last night, the same foursome gathered again by the TV, sipping *chai* and watching a local Russian language program. When Soniya left the room for a few minutes to join her mother in the kitchen, Mamluk called to me.

"*Dzhanet,*" he said, catching my eye. "We love you."
He's speaking English!

"Hadija, Soniya," and he gestured to the kitchen as he listed their names, "Fatima, Takhmina." Not knowing the word "too," he nodded and smiled and I knew he wanted to include them. He was speaking English. For me. My heart swelled and a big grin came to my face.

"*Ya toja*," (I also) I told him. "*Ya lu blu.*" My phonetic cognate, "yellow blue" made it easy for me to remember the Russian "I love you."

And I knew I did.

※

The American Embassy, at least the department I was interested in, was on the seventeenth floor of a bland bank building on the south side of Almaty.

Security was tight on the first floor: metal detectors, passport checks, purse examinations. The ritual was becoming routine. There were more hoops to get through once I got off the elevator, but it all went smoothly and soon enough I was seated comfortably across the desk of the director of the United States Consular Office.

His was an interim position, he wanted me to know, perhaps in apology for being unable to help me. He seemed not to know even about the exchange programs for locals that the Peace Corps had told us about. It didn't matter; those had proven to be competitions that were out of reach for both my students (because of their age) and my colleagues (because they were not teaching in either an elementary school or a university). College was indeed a hybrid.

As for programs to encourage Kazakhstanis to visit the States, he thought the "tourist visa" route held the best chance. Then he told me about the Edward S. Muskie Graduate Fellowship Program, available through the United States Department of State, which offered funding leading to a

161

master's degree at a US accredited college or university. It would be perfect for Gulzhahan, I thought.

We continued to chat and when I mentioned my movie night project, he told me about a grant that could let us show these movies for free. The only challenge was finding a local to serve as the lead grantee, the fancy name for the project director. That, I thought, was a perfect fit for Yulia, from my movie advisory committee.

Then, when I told him the topics I was teaching, he made a phone call and before I left I had two red-and-blue plaid rice bags overflowing with textbooks. I wasn't sure what I'd do with these single books, but I knew they would be used somehow.

Textbooks were like gold.

***

I flew back to Zhezkazgan the next day, April 27th, my son David's 32nd birthday. Woody had asked me to fly rather than take the train. It had been another one of those situations that were still far too common: I wanted A; he wanted "Not A."

"It'll be safer," he'd said. "And faster."

Eventually, he admitted he'd asked me to fly so he wouldn't worry about me. I knew I'd be exchanging two days of relative stillness for three hours of loud and incessant engine noise, but I agreed. For him. To shut him up.

My trip to Almaty had been the first time we'd been apart overnight in more than a year and I knew he would miss me; he'd said it often enough. But I wasn't so sure I would miss him; and if I did, which "him" would I be missing?

Our life together in the months since my meltdown had been more comfortable than in the months before. What helped was an exercise that I had read about while journaling and meditating by my little Chincoteague canal.

It was a simple exercise, but not easy. I'd take whatever label I was putting on Woody and apply it to myself. If I accused him of being irritable or quick-tempered, I'd experiment with, "I'm irritable or quick-tempered." Judgmental? I'd try on, "I'm judgmental." Eventually, as more of the phrases fit, I realized I had hated in him those things that I was struggling with in myself. It's such an old Life Lesson; yet there I was learning it anew at age 56.

That little exercise had shown me the part I had played in my earlier unhappiness, which had certainly led to the new harmony we were enjoying. Still, I was eager to go to Almaty when the chance arose. While there, my focus had been on the here and now: the various opportunities before me and the people I was with. I hadn't thought of Woody, let alone missed him.

I pondered these things as I gathered my luggage at the rear of the little propjet. Was I excited, eager, to see him? Or was I nervous, anxious? Physiologically, I knew, they can feel the same. *What meaning did I want to make of the flutters in my stomach?* At some point, I knew, love becomes a decision one makes, a choice. I would continue to make that choice.

Then, as I hit the tarmac and saw him waiting for me, I didn't need to search for a label. That small electric bubble of glee burst out from deep in my core.

In the early years of my life in Philadelphia, while we were still exploring a life together, each time I had seen him anew, that little electric surge screamed, "Yup; he's a keeper." It had been a long time since we'd been apart and I'd had a chance to feel that surge. But now, as I walked across the tarmac toward this broad-shouldered, white-haired man whose smile at seeing me was a mile wide, I felt it again. There was no denying—as I passed my packages to the cab driver who had brought him to meet me and fell into Woody's outstretched arms—it was back. I may not have thought of him often while I was away, but now that I was back, I was very glad to see him.

Woody was a curmudgeon; there was no denying that. I'd just not seen that side of him before. The Woody I had known over the past ten years, the one who had listened to my stories and shared his with me, the Woody I'd co-authored a textbook with, run seminars with, and shared stages with around the world had been focused, smart, introspective, and genuine. And comfortable. I'd never seen him as uncomfortable as he was in the Peace Corps. I'd known of his earlier struggles. But they were ones in the past by the time I'd met him. They no longer weighed him down like the ones he endured in Kazakhstan.

It had been easy in those early years to love Woody when all I saw of him was the strong, competent parts. Now I realized I loved the whole of him, even the part that got irritable and cranky whenever he was tired or hungry. I loved the impulsive adventurer in him that had first nudged us into joining; and I loved the judgmental Peace Corps volunteer in him that refused to go home even though he met disappointment and frustration nearly every day. Yes, I even loved the ethnocentric American who couldn't find anything to be curious about in this culture I now found fascinating. I loved him, and his curmudgeon within. And he loved me. And that was enough.

Later, as we finished the home-cooked meal Woody had prepared for me, I gazed at this man who had seemed so far away for such a very long time. He was chattering away, as he so often did, about his life while I'd been gone, and I realized we had both come back, in a way. And I couldn't help but smile.

In May, near the end of the term and just a week before Woody and I would leave for our summer vacation, I observed while the students of English 49 took their State exam. It was quite an eye-opener for me.

Gulzhahan had often said, "Grades are gifts we give our students." I had assumed she was speaking metaphorically. In my world, grades were earned. I was about to learn how grades were "given" in Kazakhstan.

When I had taught in the United States, students shuffled in for their exams in sweat suits after coffee-fueled all-nighters. Not in Kazakhstan.

I arrived a little early and walked into the exam room to find three of the best students (Gulsana, Aïda, and Mahabat) dressed in the standard formal Monday uniform of starched white blouse, black skirt, stockings and high heels, and cleaning the classroom.

"What are you doing? I asked Gulsana, who was squatted, mopping the floor with a hand-held rag.

"This is our exam room," she explained eagerly. "We want it to look nice."

And when she looked up at me, I realized I'd never seen her wearing make-up before. This was a special occasion.

Most of the desks were pushed against the back wall, with assorted maps, charts, and tables of grammar points spread out on top. "The goal here is to help the student pass," Gulzhahan told me in explanation. "If they don't pass, they may come back next year and take the exam again."

"They repeat the course?"

"No. They repeat the exam."

Five remaining desks filled the center of the room. And just inside the doorway, two long tables were pushed together lengthwise and covered in white tablecloths. Two bouquets of red roses, two cartons of juice, one bottle of mineral water, and six glasses awaited the panel of five test givers: Gulzhahan, Gulzhan, Tolganay, and two women named Bakhit—one, the college administrator I'd met on my first day; the other, an English teacher from a local secondary school. There was always a panelist from outside. And me. While I wasn't going to have any official role to play, I did get a chair, and a glass.

Each of the panelists also got a letter-size printout listing the students' names, followed by five empty columns. A seventh chair, where the student being examined would sit, sat empty on the other side of our table. I dubbed it the "hot seat."

The secretary of the college sat alone at another cloth-covered table opposite us. Her job was to watch over the array of cards that contained the examination topics.

Floors washed, tables set, furniture adjusted just so, the students of English 49 stood solemnly as the Napoleon-like director arrived for a brief opening ceremony.

Taking a pair of official-looking scissors, he cut a large envelope open and, slowly and silently, slid the numbered cards out of the envelope and handed them to the secretary. It was a somber occasion.

With great care to maintain their prearranged order, the secretary placed the cards face down on her table. Each one contained a single topic from a long list that the students had gotten ahead of time. The exam would consist of one topic from the list (the card) and one surprise grammar question.

All but five of the students filed out of the room to wait in the hallway for their turn. Gulsana, Yestai, Aïda, Zamira, and Mahabat remained, chose their cards, and announced their card's number.

"Card number 3," Aïda called out, and took a seat at one of the desks.

The five panelists marked their five-column printouts with a 3 by Aïda's name.

"Number 4," Yestai called out, and the panelists again marked their sheets. On it went.

Given the guarantee of graduation, the students' level of anxiety surprised me. I turned to Tolganay and asked, "Why are the students so nervous? We know they will pass. Surely, they know they will pass."

"They want to show how much they know. If they do poorly, they will feel bad in here," and she pointed to her heart.

166

I was also curious about all the pomp and ceremony surrounding the occasion, but I let it pass. I was there to observe, not to ask my usual "why?" I went back to my note pad.

Gulsana was first to take her place in the "hot seat." It was 9:15.

"The course of modern lexicology," she began, reading the topic on her card.

Bakhit from the other school stopped her from speaking while Dinara entered, took a card, and announced its number.

Gulsana began again, referring to notes on her lap, but Gulzhahan interrupted her.

"Do not use notes."

"The life of the modern student is…" Gulsana said, notes forgotten, and Bakhit the visiting teacher interrupted again.

"Do you want to speak English fluently?"

"Yes, of course."

"What do you do?" Bakhit asked.

I was lost as to why Bakhit was interrupting and seemingly taking Gulsana off-topic, but Gulsana did not miss a beat. "I get up at six every morning to study my…" she began, and then Bakhit interrupted with yet another question.

My irritation was growing. Why wouldn't they let her speak? She was, without a doubt, the best English speaker in the college, bar none, and an ideal student. Here was her chance to show how much she knew. I wanted her to have that chance.

"You are finished," I heard one teacher say. It was only 9:25 and Gulsana was out the door, with barely a full English sentence completed.

"Twenty more minutes," Tolganay called out to the students still earnestly writing at their desks.

"I'm confused," I said to no one in particular. "I thought they had twenty minutes."

"They have thirty minutes for state exam," Gulzhahan corrected. "Gulsana was ready early."

This didn't clarify anything for me, but I sat with my confusion rather than interrupt their process. Here was a chance for me to sit with my "wrong thumb on top," again. It was still uncomfortable.

We waited for ten minutes. Then, Yestai was in the hot seat, looking nervous. He was one of my favorite students, and I felt so proud I wanted to hug him. One of the few male students at the college, Yestai was wise and sensible. When he'd told me he wanted to go into diplomatic service for his country, I hoped that meant I would hear from him over the years. His topic was London.

"There are many centers of London," he began, sounding confident. His voice was strong, but I noticed his fingers twirling just out of sight on his lap.

"The center of London, the east end, and the west end. Hyde Park," he continued before he was cut off.

"Thank you. That is all." And he was out the door, too.

What the heck?

When the exam was over, the six judges gathered to make their final determination on "marks" and fill in the requisite forms.

There'd be no long hours at home alone slogging through handwritten essays. There'd be no mathematical calculations, no bell-curve averaging. Instead, there would be conversation and communication among these six women who needed to agree.

When they were done, the director returned to the room and looked slowly over their list of grades. Most were 5s, with a few 4s, and only two 3s. There were no 2s or 1s. The teachers watched somberly, awaiting the director's approval. They knew that if he didn't like a grade, he'd change it. Grades were, after all, gifts the director could give, too.

I left bemused. Honored that they'd allow me to sit in on such a ceremony, I was determined not to judge it. The educational system was austere, and, to me, riddled with corruption and waste. But I was not there to change the system.

I was there to make whatever difference I could in the individual lives of my students, my colleagues, and, I had to admit, me.

Chapter Sixteen
A BRIDE'S FAREWELL
AND BRIDE STEALING

In December, when Dina's younger sister Ella became engaged, she set about to organize the "bride's farewell" party. As the eldest of the parentless brood, she took her role seriously.

"When are you leaving on your holiday?" she'd asked me that winter.

When I told her we'd start our summer break on June 14, she set her sister's party for June 9. Other than my own, I'd never had a wedding party planned around my vacation schedule. By this time in our stay, I was no longer surprised by the courtesy. I was beginning to understand Kazakh rituals. And I did so, of course, by comparing them with the Western ones I knew.

American brides in generations past, for example, filled hope chests. Linens, dishes, and silver accumulated over the years, forming what we quaintly called a dowry. It's a dying custom, but based on the belief that a woman needs to bring something besides herself to the union, something material and practical to enhance her value.

In Kazakhstan, this tradition is reversed. Kazakh brides don't bring a dowry to the union. Instead, they warrant a *kalym*, literally a "bride price," a payment by the groom or his family to the bride's family before the union can occur. Whether it is meant to secure the sincerity of the groom or to replace the lost labor of the woman to her family, a *kalym*, just as a dowry taken literally, perpetuates the idea that marriage, at its core, is an economic union.

In the States, most brides still wear white and usually walk down a church aisle on the arm of their father. Does this mean most American brides are virgins when they marry, or are active churchgoers, or believe themselves property to be conveyed from father to husband? Certainly not. These 21st-century wedding traditions are generally no longer taken literally. But since I was an outsider observing the Kazakh traditions around marriage, I didn't know how literally Kazakhs took their rituals.

When Dina told me that Ella and her young man were looking for an apartment and she planned to furnish it, I was curious.

"What about Ella's *kalym?*" I asked.

"They will give us jewelry," was all she would say.

One spring day, I learned more on one of my walks with Kamshat, a colleague who lived just beyond my apartment and often walked me home. She was one of the younger teachers, and a woman who'd made a point of meeting as many Peace Corps volunteers over the years as she could. Her English was, probably as a result, quite good and I'd learned a lot from her during our many talks.

Over the next few months, as Dina proceeded with the plans for Ella's wedding, I took the opportunity to ask Kamshat about Kazakh wedding traditions.

"When a daughter marries," she told me, "she is considered no longer part of her own family but part of the family of her husband."

Was this behind Dina's frequent rush of tears as June drew close?

"And if she marries the youngest son in a family," Kamshat continued, "she moves into the home of her husband's parents, where her husband lives."

A Kazakh tradition traced back to Genghis Khan in the thirteenth century, the youngest son has the responsibility of caring for his parents until their deaths. Of course, mothers tend to outlive fathers, even in Central Asia, so the new wife is often considered her mother-in-law's maid.

I wondered what my daughter-in-law, Jenna, now on her way to a master's degree in nursing and married to my younger son, Jon, would have to say about foregoing her higher education to spend her life catering to me. I felt quite certain the idea would not go over well.

My walks with Kamshat taught me aspects of Kazakh culture I didn't talk about with my students.

"You're an only child." I asked on another walk. "Will you take care of your mother, too?"

"If a mother has only a daughter, when she gets old, she is out of luck."

I thought of the elderly woman who stood begging inside the *pochta* every day. Was it that she had no sons? I asked Kamshat about her.

"Some mothers move in with the daughters," she explained, "but only if the son-in-law and his parents agree."

Then, after a few minutes of silence, she continued.

"Sometimes the daughter fixes her mother's meals or cleans for her. Of course, his mother will always come first."

Finally, she addressed my question about the woman at the *pochta*.

"Her children have probably moved away."

Later that same week, I took another walk with my colleague Tolganay, who had agreed to help me track down the marvelous smell of freshly baked bread in a neighborhood with no apparent stores. The scent was such a mystery that our search took longer than we'd expected. Conversation came easily and soon the topic was husbands. I wanted to see if Kamshat's stories would match Tolganay's.

"If you had two boyfriends, one was an older son, the other the youngest, whom would you rather marry?" I asked.

I expected her to think about it a bit. Maybe mention love. Instead, without a moment's pause, she responded.

"The older." Then she laughed. "I wouldn't want all the work of being married to a youngest brother."

Tolganay was in fact married to an oldest son, but his younger brothers were not yet married. So, as the sole daughter-in-law, after each day at work, she'd go to her in-law's home, fix dinner and clean the house. Then she'd go home to do the same.

"It is my duty," she said, with no sense of an injustice.

These "rules" were so fixed, so firm, that no one seemed to question them. There was no room for a devil's advocate, debate, or alternative viewpoints. So I didn't offer any.

❧❦❧

When June finally came, Woody and I found ourselves in a party center decorated with colorful streamers and full of people dressed elegantly in bright colors. This was Ella's farewell party.

Farewell parties for brides are a recent addition to the Kazakh culture. Gulzhahan, for example, as the youngest, was the only one of her four sisters to have a farewell party.

"They weren't done when my sisters got married," she explained to me, not needing to explain yet another prohibition under the Soviet system, another change that had come with independence.

When Woody and I arrived, we spotted Dina quickly. She hugged us and took us immediately to meet her two brothers, who were standing alone off to the side and dressed in suits and ties. They looked like they could think of many things they'd rather be doing, but they shook Woody's hands in the traditional two-handed shake of Islam and nodded a friendly *"D'rast*

174

v'witchya" to me. Women in Kazakhstan don't shake hands, certainly not with men.

Dinner was *bishparmak*, which was no surprise. Rather than beef or mutton, though, horse was the meat of choice for this festive, formal occasion.

As is customary, the *bishparmak* platter came to the table with the meat in huge chunks. A man from the kitchen staff was assigned to cut it up and serve it, a man with the blackest fingernails we'd ever seen. Woody and I would not be eating any.

Of course, he could have been an auto mechanic with permanently stained but clean fingers. Or not. Fortunately, Togzhan, a friend from my movie advisory committee and also a friend and former classmate of Dina's other sister Gulmira, had also noticed.

"Just leave it on your plate," she advised quietly. "Push it over to the side. But take it."

I was hungry and the food looked so good. But neither Woody nor I could get past the fingernails. The multiple salads on the table and the rice on the platter would hold me until the second meal that would come near midnight, maybe *ploff* (rice pilaf) or *galupsi* (stuffed cabbage). I was feeling rather pleased that I'd been to enough of these to know the routine, but also rather self-conscious of my elevated sense of fastidiousness.

Ella was radiant in a pale green satin gown, and her groom, looking far too young to marry, was appropriately handsome and happy. They sat under a canopied table in a corner far across the dance floor from the guests, with two similarly attired attendants at their side.

There was a happy hum of conversation all around and live music while we ate. This could have been a wedding party in the States but, when it was over, Ella would join her fiancé's family until the wedding.

Would they share a bed? How could I even ask such a question?

The toasts began during dinner. Proclaiming the truly unique value of an individual takes a long time. No one holds a glass on high during these extended monologues and proclaims a simple "congratulations and best wishes." That is practically insulting. A toast is more like a eulogy, but a eulogy to the future.

Since Woody and I did not imbibe and neither of us knew much Kazakh beyond my mangled *Sally misses beer* (hello) and my new favorite, *sour bones* (good-bye), we'd found the 1950s era song, *Magic Penny*, worked well as our toast, particularly at such a large, formal event as this one.

We'd sung it first at my colleague Raisa's birthday, a small affair in her home. And it had been met with such enthusiasm that we kept doing it at each opportunity to offer a toast. The melody was a straightforward, simple one and we particularly liked the message of the chorus:

Love is something, if you give it away ... you end up having more.

There were many verses and we varied the presentation from time to time by singing different ones.

It's just like a magic penny, hold it tight and you won't have any. Lend it, spend it and you'll have so many, they'll roll all over the floor. So ...

Festivities that last past nine o'clock are torture for Woody. And that night he left shortly after the meal was served and before the toasts were finished, the "sudden illness" he used by way of explanation brought on only by the late hour. Two unknown young men escorted him home, a common practice I appreciated, though Woody deemed it a silly custom. But with my partner gone, I'd not planned to sing the toast on my own. Unfortunately, I hadn't conveyed to anyone that I'd sit this one out. Silly me.

As if on cue, the room went quiet and I realized eyes were on me, staring expectantly. Togzhan, sitting next to me, urged me forward.

"You need to toast," she told me. "It's your turn."

Who knew there were turns?

No problem. I would sing *Magic Penny* by myself. Sing out, my New York City singing coach Susan Gregory had taught me back in 2002 when I'd taken lessons with her, the fulfillment of a lifelong dream. "Sing out so I can hear you," she'd said. "I can't fix it if I can't hear it."

Ambling slowly to the microphone, I realized I couldn't quite remember the words. *No problem*, I told myself. *The words will come to me once I begin to sing.*

I took the microphone in my hand and waited expectantly for the opening line to come to me, something about love.

"Love is la, la, la," I sang out, followed with more, "La, la, la."

The melody didn't sound quite right either. Still, I was not feeling the panic I'd felt at age eight when I ran from the room and locked myself in the bathroom after making a mistake playing the piano in front of strangers. No. This time I'd just keep at it. Progress, not perfection, was my mantra, the same one I'd been preaching to my students. Sing out, I'd told them, metaphorically anyway. Now, I told myself again, sing out; the words and music will come.

I started and stopped a few more times but neither the lyrics nor the melody came to me.

The guests, some 500 of them, were clapping, laughing, enjoying my crazy little show, it seemed. Honestly, I could have read the Manhattan telephone book and they'd have still appreciated me. Then the applause began to sound more like an invitation to finish up and get off the stage, one of those rhythmic beats where everyone claps to the same cadence, urging me to "get on with it, enough already."

So, I simply said, "I wish you both a long and happy life," handed the microphone back to the hired emcee, turned to return to my seat, and bumped directly into Dina. She was there with gifts: a blue Kazakh vest for me, and a green Kazakh robe for Woody. We hadn't done anything.

After more toasts, it was time for Ella's family to say goodbye. This was a Farewell Party, after all. Dina, Gulmira, their two brothers, and assorted aunts and uncles stood in a straight line at the microphone. Their toasts took over an hour and were, of course, in Kazakh. Their voices were subdued and there was no laughter. Togzhan translated occasionally, but it didn't matter. Their body language spoke openly of their sorrow.

Then Ella's two sisters-in-law unrolled a white runner across the front of the room to the door. They sprinkled flower petals over it, then guided Ella and her fiancé along it and through the door to her future husband's family.

The actual wedding, with only the groom's family and friends in attendance, would be two days later, and another huge party would follow. The groom's family would do the inviting to that one and we were not included. Neither was Dina.

As I watched from a few tables away, Dina broke down in sobs.

Not all brides glow on their wedding day.

I first heard about bride abduction during training when Mamluk wouldn't let his adult daughters go into Almaty alone, and I'd asked my inevitable "Why?" Soniya had grabbed the front of her blouse, giving a pulling motion. When I didn't understand, she took my dictionary and looked up the English word, "to steal."

At the time, I chalked it up to an overprotective father and promptly forgot about it. *Surely, men here did not steal girls off the street and marry them, the same street where I, or any woman, could flag down a passing car and negotiate the price of a lift.* Turns out, they can; and they do.

Aktigul, one of my quieter students who sat in the back row of English 30 throughout the year, was the first of my students to be stolen. There would be too many. One Monday morning I remarked that she was missing.

"She'll be back next week," other students said.

"Where did she go?" I asked.

"She was stolen," they said, matter-of-factly.

I was dumbfounded.

"Where were the girl's parents? Why didn't they go get her?"

"They were there," my students assured me in their rudimentary English.

Surely I was missing something.

I brought the subject up in my stronger English 49 class, on a day when we had a smaller group than usual. I thought with both Gulsana and Yestai absent, the remaining female students might speak more freely.

"What's bride stealing?" I asked them. "I just learned one of my students has been stolen. Why can't I call the police?"

"That won't help," I heard repeated across the room. "She won't complain."

"She knows him," a voice called out from the back row. "He plans it." And I heard the disdain in her voice. "He decides who he wants, then plans how to steal her."

The realization that bride stealing wasn't random brought me little relief.

"Where are the boy's parents?" I demanded, naively. My students assured me they, or at least his mother, were right there waiting at home for the man to show up with his stolen woman. And his grandmother if he had one, and aunts, and sisters, and all the female relatives that could fit in the house.

"Aktigul was stolen by her boyfriend's friend," came a voice from the front.

"Sometimes," my students explained, "he's an old boyfriend."

"Sometimes she doesn't even know him at all," came another voice.

"How does he do it?" I asked, incredulous.

"Well, he doesn't do it alone," someone off to the right said.

"Yes," came a chorus of voices. "He always has friends."

"Well, how does the poor girl get inside the car? Do they put a bag over her head?"

"Maybe. Sometimes. Usually she accepts a ride to a party. Then they go to his house."

So it's usually arranged ahead of time, under the guise of giving her a lift. And, once in the car, he drives to a party all right: a wedding party at his parents' house. I was starting to get the picture.

"It's like he takes her on a date," called out a normally quiet student at the back.

Through the eighty minutes we had for our class, the story of how bride stealing was returning to Kazakhstan since independence came spilling out of the mouths of my students. But still I felt confused, numb.

"Where are the girl's parents?" I asked.

"They are there."

"From the beginning?" I was aghast. This was too much.

"They get called," said one student.

"Sometimes they already know," another added.

I was intrigued. I expected to hear that the parents were called, came, and took their daughter back home with them, irate at the least, and certainly filing charges with the local police. But I heard another scenario instead.

"The parents ask their daughter if she will marry," one student reported.

"She has to say yes," said another.

I couldn't get past my post-women's-liberation interpretation of this. Each of these young girls, generally not yet out of college, has lived her whole life with her parents. Now, she is faced with the choice of living with a man who has abducted her against her will or... Or what?

Too often, her parents won't let her come back home to live with them. *Where would she live? How would she live? No wonder these girls rarely say "no."*

"So what happens when she says yes?" I asked my students. "Does it mean there's no *kalym*?"

"No."

180

This was no moneysaving venture, my students assured me. Once the girl has agreed to marry, it's as though no one had stolen anyone. There's still the kalym to pay and, though it's very unusual, there may even be a farewell party given if the bride's mother insists. It would, of course, come after the wedding.

English was pouring out of my students' mouths, telling me stories of abductions they each knew about, when one of my more outgoing students, Mahabat, walked into the room, quite late.

Grasping the conversation while she strode to her desk— my students had finally stopped interrupting class with the customary and overly formal "may I come in" at the door—she made an announcement.

"If someone steals me, I'm outta there." Thrilling to hear, but none of the other students believed her.

"You won't leave," said a chorus of female voices. If she went home to her parents, they insisted, she'd be a marked woman. "No one else will ever marry you," they chimed.

"If my parents came to the man's home and I said I didn't want to marry him, my parents would say 'bye, bye' to me." This was Dinara, Mahabat's best friend.

"I don't care. I'm outta there," Mahabat retorted. "My mother told me I don't have to stay."

So, this was something mothers cautioned their daughters about; that was encouraging. I turned back to my class, eager for specifics.

"What if a girl has a boyfriend who's in Astana studying to be a doctor? They plan to marry but have decided to wait until he's finished with his studies." These were the details of Aktigul's situation, as I understood them.

"She's walking down the street, on the way to the store to buy milk. A car pulls up with a man who takes her and announces his intention to marry her."

"How old is he?" someone called out, lightheartedly.

"He's old," I said, wanting this to be clear-cut.

"If he's wealthy, I'm his," someone shouted from the back and the class laughed.

"What if he's poor?" I countered, adopting their lighthearted tone. "And," I threw in for good measure, "ugly."

To a one, even Mahabat, each of my students was convinced that once the girl was stolen, even if her parents took her back, her boyfriend in Astana would never marry her.

Surely, I'd misunderstood something.

Later that night, I searched the Internet from my laptop and did some reading. Apparently, in nomadic times, bride abduction was not unlike elopement. It was a way for young lovers to marry in the face of parental opposition, a way for a daughter to escape an arranged marriage she didn't want, or a way for the groom to bypass paying the *kalym*. In any case, bride stealing in nomadic times was generally consensual.

Under the Soviets, the practice was officially banned, as were other Kazakh traditions. Marriage under Communist rule was a civil matter, accomplished with two simple signatures in a registry. Then, with independence, came a resurgence of Kazakh pride and the return of old traditions into everyday life. Unfortunately, this one had come back oddly mutated.

Consensual bride abduction, where the woman was willing but unaware of the when and where of her abduction, had existed below the radar throughout Soviet times. But non-consensual bride abduction—bride stealing, the term my colleagues and students used—was on the rise.

Old boyfriends, my students had told me, were generally the culprits, or those afraid they'd soon become an "old boyfriend." According to a number of articles, abductors are often young men who are afraid they might become a rejected boyfriend. In any case, the man not only knows the woman, he knows who her ancestors were back seven generations. It is, indeed, planned.

Then I read interviews with abducted women who reported being happy now that they were settled in their new life. They may have fought and screamed at the start, but they insisted they weren't screaming now. I found it all fascinating.

Stockholm syndrome? I read on.

The groom and his cohorts may do the initial abduction, but compared to what comes next, their job seems relatively benign. It falls to the women in the boy's family to convince the girl to marry their boy, a task that often takes all night, sometimes days. It is her destiny, they tell her, her obligation to marry their son, brother, nephew, whatever he is. They need her to agree, for the Imam will later ask the woman if she's entering the marriage willingly.

Once the girl consents, and I was beginning to understand that the odds were that she would, her family is contacted. Then things get even more bizarre.

The girl's parents, I read, often believe the marriage is their daughter's destiny, the will of Allah. In fact, in a survey of local people, most Kazakhs believe bride stealing in general should be illegal, but if the girl is taken, she should stay and marry. A few girls do refuse, but only a very few. Surely, whether they give in or stand firm, their lives are forever changed.

I closed up my computer and thought of Aktigul. *Did she fight? Did she scream? Would she be happy?*

I couldn't imagine.

PART III

Wherever you are happy, you can call that home.
Dalai Lama (1935 -)

Chapter Seventeen
SUMMER VACATION

Woody and I eagerly anticipated a break from the fast pace and unremitting strangeness of that first year.

We'd accumulated enough vacation days to plan a fourteen-day rendezvous in Denmark with my son Jon and his family. This would be followed by a three-week stint as Peace Corps trainers for the next batch of English teacher volunteers. Then we'd head to Esik for a short visit with Hadija and her family before taking the train to the northern part of the country where Woody would work on his Russian with a special tutor and I'd get a jump on my movie night vocabulary lists. Plans intact, we went blissfully into our summer.

We arrived in Copenhagen a few hours ahead of Jon and Jenna, and I waited as anxiously and eagerly as only a mother—and grandmother—can. Finally, I heard their flight announced and we made our way to the international gate.

I stood off to one side as passenger after passenger emerged through the double doors. Suddenly, there was Mikah, my five-year-old grandson, holding his dad's hand. He saw me the same moment I saw him, and bolted straight for me. I knelt down on one knee to receive him so I wouldn't get bowled over in his exuberance. My vacation had begun.

Mikah's hug was filled with five-year-old excitement—or was it the release of energy after too many hours bottled up on an airplane? I didn't care and it didn't matter. Jon was there next with a weary hug for me, then one for Woody. I'd long marveled at how welcoming both my sons had been when Woody entered my life. The men in my life seemed to genuinely enjoy each other.

"Where's Jenna?" I asked Jon after Mikah and I had settled into a comfortable standing snuggle. I'd been aware of her absence, along with eighteen-month old Isabella, my granddaughter.

Jon nodded to an alcove below a staircase nearby. I walked over to find Jenna standing in front of a hysterically screaming Bella, who was perched on a counter. Jenna stood in front of her at Bella's elevated eye-level trying to calm her. They must have slipped past me while I'd been focused on Mikah and Jon.

I stood in the opening of the alcove and smiled to Jenna, who nodded in reply, then returned her attention to Bella.

"It's OK. You're fine. We're here." Her soothing voice was calmly repeating these words. But Isabella would have none of it. And I got the impression Jenna was reminding herself, as well, that the long, grueling flight was over.

While Jenna and Isabella coped together with what had been a difficult flight, Jon and Woody set out to collect the luggage and find us a taxi large enough to hold four adults, two children, one car seat, and way more bags than should ever be needed. It didn't take long, and soon enough we were piled in an eight-passenger van, our possessions secured in the back.

Jenna had found the rental house, a typically attractive ranch house in the Danish suburb of Ishoj, through the Internet. Situated mid-way between a twenty-minute walk to the train into Copenhagen and a twenty-minute walk in the other direction to the beach, it was perfect. There were two bedrooms, a large eat-in kitchen, and a living room with sliding glass doors that overlooked a lush, green backyard lined with hedges of ripe rhubarb that went all the way to a marshy bay.

"Fresh rhubarb!" I cried with delight at the sight of a fresh vegetable at my fingertips. My regular Kazakh fare of parsley and dill had gotten old and I'd craved fresh vegetables for far too long.

While the other adults in our group unpacked, Mikah and I took Bella for a walk through the backyard and harvested so much rhubarb that after only a few days of "another dish of rhubarb," none of us wanted to see it again. Such was our first day.

We spent the rest of our days frequenting the nearby beach, exploring the small town center, and seeing the typical tourist stops in Copenhagen: Tivoli Garden, the changing of the guard at Amalienborg Palace, the many fine restaurants along the renovated harbor where I ate my fill of smoked herring, a languorous cruise among the canals, and a glimpse of the Little Mermaid lounging on a rock—a replica of the Hans Christian Anderson character which looked mighty lifelike, if unexpectedly tiny.

One lazy afternoon, on our walk to the beach, I watched as Jon challenged Mikah to a "sword fight" with reeds from a nearby marsh. Cries of *en guarde* filled the air, and their laughter tugged at my heart. I loved seeing Jon so happy.

This visit, I'd realize only later, was the longest span of time Jon and I had been together since I'd moved away ten years before. The only thing that would have made me happier in that moment was having David and his family there, too. But Dave's wife was not the traveling sort and he'd said no to our invitation. I missed them. In Kazakhstan, I'd seen what large extended families looked like and how important they were to the people there. They'd become important to me too. I suddenly wanted my extended family around me.

At the beach, Woody and I sat on a blanket and watched while Jon and Jenna took the kids into the frigid water. *Why was no one cold?* Woody and Jon were comfortable in the Danish breezes and Jenna wore tank tops each day. But my body, now used to the high heat of Kazakhstan, needed time to adjust. I wore turtlenecks and thick cotton sweaters.

On other days, we visited a nearby Viking museum and took a side trip into Sweden. But my favorite times involved simply rolling on the living room floor with Mikah and Bella, riding them on my knees, mock wrestling, and having tickling matches. I absolutely loved to hear them laugh.

Our ten days together went by too fast and soon enough it was over, time for Jon and his family to fly back home to Ohio and for Woody and me to fly back to Kazakhstan. The visit had been filled with good food, a little luxury, chilly weather, and family: things Woody and I would miss back in Zhezkazgan. I said goodbye with a wistful feeling in my heart.

Seeing my grandchildren again had reminded me of my place in the larger circle of life. The family I'd helped to create danced to their own drummer, but they included me in their song. How unlike the tight but extensive families I knew in Kazakhstan.

If we were Kazakh, Jon—as my younger son—and Jenna would be living with me, destined to care for me for the rest of my life. I smiled, realizing that although I missed my various family members, I still preferred my more independent American way: separate, individual lives, coming together now and then, in and out, like an accordion.

The trip to Copenhagen was the first time I'd been out of Kazakhstan since we'd arrived the year before, and I saw firsthand how negative the European attitudes about the country were, and how little is known of Kazakhstan in the West. While we were traveling, whenever Woody or I mentioned where we now lived, people often expressed sympathy for us. The beautician who gave me a spiky haircut in Copenhagen actually rolled her eyes.

The Danes knew of Kazakhstan's pervasive corruption, her crumbling infrastructure, the greedy privatization of her natural resources, and the devastating nuclear pollution around the former Soviet testing site. I'd been critical of these things, too, at the beginning. They were legitimate problems, after all.

But in Denmark, that's all they knew, and I found myself defending the country I was slowly growing to love. I saw Kazakhstan's problems as byproducts of the Soviet's seventy-year reign, rather than choices of the people who lived there and now ruled. I wanted to shout at the beautician and the many others who'd given similar reactions, "The Soviets haven't destroyed Kazakh hospitality. They haven't killed the great sense of fun and good humor my friends there have. And they certainly haven't affected the Kazakh ability to accept the unacceptable with grace and dignity."

I wanted to tell the hairdresser that despite the hundreds of nuclear tests on Kazakh soil that had decimated the bird and bug population, the Soviets hadn't marred the bright, sunny weather I so loved. I wanted the world to know this Kazakhstan.

By the time I left Denmark, I vowed to find a way to change the world's view of the country I'd so recently misunderstood myself.

I was glad to be back in Kazakhstan. Following our three weeks of work at the Peace Corps' training site, we headed to the village of Esik, just outside of Almaty, for a short visit with Hadija and Mamluk and their family. At least that had been the plan. But when Woody's wallet was stolen at a bus stop in Almaty, our brief visit turned into a month while we waited for the replacements of our various cards to be mailed to the Peace Corps' safer diplomatic mailbox in nearby Almaty.

We were lucky, I thought, to have the loss of the wallet happen while we were already settled at Hadija's. We could still save our remaining vacation days. I'd work on my vocabulary handouts and Woody could practice his Russian with the family.

We'd just do these things in the south, in Esik, rather than in the north, as planned.

My two visits to the family over the past year had been short ones, tacked onto the beginning of a longer visit to Almaty for ongoing training by the Peace Corps (in the winter) or the NATEK conference (in the spring). This visit, now expanded by the need to replace stolen credit cards in a country with a challenging postal system, would be more like our initial stay the summer before. Maybe better, since we'd not be away all day at training. I looked forward to what I thought would be lots of time to visit with the family and still get my work done. And that's just how it started out.

One night after dinner, we all walked the two blocks to visit Mamluk's mother for dinner. She was a heavyset woman, with the traditional headscarf and a quick, friendly smile. Though we never spoke directly, I always felt welcomed by her.

After dinner, Mamluk wandered outside with his younger brother—who, of course, lived there with his family—while Hadija, Woody, and I settled in with *chai* around the table as the daughters from both families cleared the table.

Soon enough, Soniya and her sister Fatima snuggled up with their *babushka* (grandmother) on the sofa. I appreciated the warmth in their relationships. What mostly-grown granddaughters would cuddle with their elders in the States?

Mamluk's widowed German sister-in-law was also visiting. She spoke English and Woody tried to engage her in the German he once knew, though she kept responding to him in English. Having her there was more fortuitous than I imagined for Soniya had, inexplicably, stopped speaking English to us.

The *babushka* wanted to tell us a story. As the German daughter-in-law translated, we realized it was a story about her arrival in Kazakhstan. It was a sad tale, and one that the family had heard many times it seemed, as Soniya would often chide her into adding another bit that she'd left out.

We learned of the long train ride with no seats, no heat, no food, and many people dying along the way. She had been only five when she came, yet she did not seem sad as she told her story, just matter-of-fact.

Then she began to chuckle as she told us about a chest full of jewelry her family had left behind. Her father was a jeweler and, before they were forced out of their home for the arduous journey to a strange new land, he collected his inventory, put it in a small chest, and buried it in the back yard.

"Somewhere in Georgia, someone has become very rich," she said through her daughter-in-law, laughing.

She was the first person I'd met who'd actually been part of a history I'd only read about—the "reign of terror" under Joseph Stalin—when entire populations were uprooted and dispersed to foreign lands, or, worse, to gulags.

Her loss saddened me. Her story touched my heart and I wanted them to know. I wanted the connection that comes with shared grief. But no one else appeared sad and I couldn't find a way to make them understand. It was another moment when I deeply regretted not knowing Russian better. And once the sister-in-law left and Soniya's English reticence continued, there would be many more.

Over the many weeks we were there, I didn't see Hadija very much. For one thing, I was buried in my movie project, creating the vocabulary list for *You've Got Mail*, the Tom Hanks and Meg Ryan comedy that was to open our second season.

Some nights Fatima pulled dinner together, and some nights Woody and I went out to eat. Life was easygoing and relaxed, except when I wanted to ask something specific—like, Where was Hadija?—and found teen-aged Soniya adamantly refusing to speak English. I was so confused by her change in attitude and, trying not to take it personally, I initially chalked it up to adolescent obstinacy and wished we'd thought to pack our dictionary.

Eventually, it did hurt. "I won't speak to you anymore in Russian until you speak to me in English," I snapped at her one day. It did nothing to help, of course, and she just looked at me.

Woody talked to her in Russian and reported, "Her sisters are uncomfortable when she speaks English."

That's what Soniya had told him, but I didn't believe it. They weren't petty girls and they hadn't minded Soniya's English during our previous summer. So as Soniya walked with me into town one afternoon with no sisters around, I raised the subject again in my hybrid Russian-English mix.

"I miss talking to you," I told her after apologizing for snapping. "It's hard for me. You were so helpful last summer. What happened?"

"I don't know words," she admitted, stumbling a bit. Her long dark ponytail hung limply down her back.

It was the first English I'd heard from her since we'd arrived.

"I can't speak if I don't know words."

Perfectionism again! Was it possible that in just one year it had gotten a hold of her? She was thinner than I remembered, too, unlike her sisters. But then, she'd always been different from them, more adventurous, daring. I didn't see that anymore.

I'd found perfectionism rampant among my students and colleagues, often paralyzing them. Perfectionism wasn't unique to Kazakhs, of course. Indeed, I'd found it a universal curse, one that had once affected me as well. I understood what Soniya was struggling with. But her struggle was affecting our visit tremendously. We continued our walk together, bonded at least by honesty, if not English.

"Do you think I'm a perfectionist?" I asked Woody later in our room.

"In what way?"

He smiled that disarming smile that told me that, even if I were, he'd long ago made peace with it.

"I'm wondering if it's what keeps me from immersing myself in Russian. I'm thinking of Soniya not speaking English."

"No. You're actually great at speaking Russian badly."

He looked at me for the hearty laugh he expected but saw I was serious.

"What keeps us both from learning Russian," and now he too was serious, "is that we're surrounded by English."

***

The mystery of Hadija's long absences was solved when I wandered up the road to her mother's house, a place I'd visited many times during our first summer.

As I walked into the courtyard, I saw that Hadija and all four of her sisters were gathered at their childhood home, making *pelmini* (Russian raviolis) in the outdoor kitchen. Only three sisters lived in Esik. The other two I'd never met before and all were together now, I quickly learned, for that ancient rite of passage: the deathwatch. I'd had no idea.

I walked over to stand by their mother who lay behind a curtain. She was propped up on a bed filled with pillows and as her eyes met mine, I smiled. *Kak dila* (how are you), my usual Russian greeting, was utterly inappropriate and I had nothing else to say. I didn't even know her name.

I turned to watch the sisters. As one rolled out the sheets of homemade noodles, another cut them into small squares, and the other three filled each square with a small dollop of meat, then pinched the sides together.

In that pantomime way of communication that Hadija and I had perfected, the sisters encouraged me to join them. Without hesitation, I joined the fill-and-pinch station. My *pelmini* were sad-looking, haphazard concoctions that often needed to be rescued, but no one minded. How I wished I could understand what they were saying as they worked together in solidarity.

Because this was a sad time for Hadija and her family and because of my inability to communicate in any substantive way, the contrast in our two summers with Hadija was significant.

I found some respite from my language-related isolation, and would learn just how different this visit was for the family, too, when Gulzhahan arrived from Zhezkazgan. She'd come for her three-week stint in the training of the new Peace Corps group. But before it started, and knowing we were somewhere in Esik, she took a bus from Almaty and came to find us. Thanks to our cell phones, she did. She and Hadija had met, of course, at the train station when we first left for Zhezkazgan. Now she would meet the rest of the family.

"Any friend of yours is welcome here," Mamluk told us at the table that afternoon, and I believed him. I also understood his Russian.

Hadija's home was run much like an American home in that we made ourselves at home rather than expecting to be waited on. But this was not the Kazakh way. Gulzhahan, unsure how to be a good guest under those circumstances, did her best.

That afternoon, as Gulzhahan sat with Hadija and me sipping our afternoon *chai*, Hadija and Gulzhahan conversed in Russian while I tried to catch a word here and there. When Gulzhahan translated for me what Hadija was saying, I was not only surprised, I was crushed.

"Janet worked hard last summer, Hadija was saying. This summer, she doesn't work so hard."

Gulzhahan stated this to me calmly and with no trace of embarrassment on my behalf. I couldn't quite believe I was hearing her right. I sat still, wavering between feeling embarrassed and insulted. My face turned hot, my heart started beating quickly, and the room took on an eerie silence. And then Hadija went on. I was almost afraid to imagine what would be next.

"Janet cooked for us last summer. This summer she doesn't cook. This is her lazy summer."

Although Hadija laughed when she said it, her words stung through Gulzhahan's straightforward translation. *What didn't I understand?*

I thought I knew the way the family operated: make yourself at home, take care of yourself, don't be a burden. But somehow, something had been expected of me that I didn't know about. And I'd missed the cues. I no longer had Soniya to run language interference for me, and Woody had given up on engaging anyone in Russian.

I was alone in trying to communicate. *Was I needed in some way I didn't understand because of Hadija's mother's illness? Were they giving off clues I couldn't perceive?*

Our first summer, I'd gone off all day, five days a week, sometimes six, to work at the Peace Corps training site. This summer I'd spent most of my time at my laptop working on the *You've Got Mail* vocabulary handout.

I must have watched the classic comedy of cross-country love half a dozen times to determine which words would need defining for my students. I realized that Hadija saw me sitting at my computer each day watching a movie. For all she knew, I was eating bonbons and sipping *mai tais*. Was that it?

Maybe the problem was financial. The Peace Corps had paid our rent that first summer, though we never knew how much. For this visit, there was no such arrangement. We were there as guests who perhaps had overstayed their welcome. We'd given the family money toward groceries, about what we'd given Dina, and we planned to give her more after we'd gotten our various bankcards replaced. But they didn't know that. *Perhaps she thought we were taking advantage of her.*

I'd once felt so close to Hadija. I thought we had an understanding, a connection that seemed to transcend our many differences. I wanted that connection back and I didn't know how to get it. I sat with my sadness for the rest of the day. As I walked Gulzhahan back to the bus stop that evening, I was grateful she didn't mention it. She wouldn't, of course. Negative, difficult, painful topics were rarely mentioned. *How Kazakh of her.* And with that thought, I realized I was reacting as an American.

Words hurt. American schoolyard bullies have known that for generations. But that's not how it works in Kazakhstan. Hadija did not intend to hurt me. Her words of criticism were no different from those of my colleagues when they announced that Gulzhahan was a bad cook, which she was.

Gulzhahan had laughed it off at the time. I needed to, too. It wouldn't be easy, but I would try to trust my relationship with Hadija instead of interpreting it through my American lenses. I would resign myself to the fact that this might very well be my "lazy summer."

❧❦❧

Four days after Hadija's mother died, Woody's credit cards arrived at the Peace Corps office. We boarded the local bus into Almaty to pick them up and book our return flight to Zhezkazgan.

It had been a long summer, a tiring vacation in many ways, and getting back to our apartment in our little town held great appeal. We said a sad farewell to Hadija and her family, not knowing when or even if we'd see them again, and moved to a hotel in Almaty for our final evening, closer to the airport.

Woody doesn't feel calm when we're traveling unless he gets to whatever gate he's going through hours before he needs to. So, after checking our bags with the airline, we settled in at a Nescafe red café where we could keep an eye on our departure gate.

With hours to kill, I dug out my journal as Woody opened the book he was currently reading. American pop music blared disconcertingly in the background.

As I opened my frayed notebook, I saw my list that Gulzhahan and I had been working on over the past six months or so, a list we called "Cultural Differences in the Classroom." It reminded me that, as I moved into my second year, I knew more of what to expect.

While I'd been so quick to notice the oddities and strange practices among my Kazakh colleagues that first year, Gulzhahan had been equally diligent to let me know that the identification of odd "cultural differences" went both ways. I smiled as I looked over our list, remembering the question I'd posed to her one afternoon in the school's café.

"What do I do that seems strange to you?"

It turned out that my "flipping them the bird" every time I pointed to a word on the blackboard had been only the beginning. It was not enough to chalk the differences up to the individualistic culture (mine) versus communal culture (hers). We wanted concrete examples of these differences. So, we started our list.

My water bottle was a case in point. For years, I'd taken for granted that sipping water throughout the day, especially in hot weather, was a good thing. Unfortunately, the sips I'd taken in Kazakhstan during my lectures weren't viewed as healthy. Rather it signaled I was "undisciplined and self-indulgent." Kazakh teachers never drink during a lesson—water on a hot day, coffee on a cold day, even the ever-present *chai*—in front of their students.

When I sat on the classroom desk, or, to be more accurate, leaned against it to give my weak back a little respite, I might well have been perceived as sacrilegious.

"Table tops are holy," Gulzhahan had told me early on. "It's where we may eat. We would never sit on one." It had taken me months to absorb the idea that this taboo included any surface that might ever be used as a *dastarkhan* (a table top), a teacher's desk included.

Kazakh teachers never count their students. During one of my early team-teaching classes with Gulzhahan, I began counting the students by twos, needing to know how many chocolate bars to hand out. Gulzhahan stopped me.

"Counting is only for animals," she had explained.

"How do you know how many there are?" I'd asked, baffled.

"We take attendance."

I was proud of my collaboration with Gulzhahan. Neither of us was trying to convert the other. Indeed, the idea never occurred to us that either of us was wrong. We were simply curious about our differences, often laughing at the absurdity of some of them. Our intent was to learn, to understand, to grow as human beings, and, hopefully, to try to find a way to expand our process to include other cultures, other classrooms, other teachers.

We both loved our own culture and understood the larger role that culture plays. It shows us where we belong and binds us to those who are like us. But sharing a culture can also set us apart from those who are different, creating outsiders, aliens, the ominous "other."

We were a well-suited duo to tackle this challenge. Gulzhahan and I trusted each other, talked to each other, and were eager to answer each other's questions without judgment.

At the same time, I had never felt judged by anyone there. Through naiveté and ignorance, I'd made multiple *faux pas*, and each one had been met with understanding, patience, and not a little resignation. I remembered a student in one of the classes that first semester after I'd learned about pointing. I'd had much trouble remembering to not point. Something I'd done so habitually, so unconsciously for so many years was hard to stop. I'd turned to my students and let them know.

"It's hard for me to remember," I had told them. "I'm hoping you are not too offended when I forget."

A student along the far wall, one of the stronger students, responded.

"It's okay. You're an American. We're used to it."

Sitting in the airport's bright red café, I chuckled as I remembered how I'd felt when I finally used my pen as a pointer: as though I were putting on airs. I'd ignored my internal affectation-alert and just kept on. *How would I fare with the pointer this second year? Would it still feel like an affectation?* I was eager to find out.

Our boarding call pulled me out of my reverie, and I realized how eager I was to get on board, to get back to our town, our work, and to my friend Gulzhahan and our shared vision. I was going home, home to my life in Zhezkazgan.

Home to the Kazakh steppe.

Chapter Eighteen
HOME IN ZHEZKAZGAN

I expected our second year to be different from our first, and I was not disappointed. Not only had our country director said as much during training, it just made intuitive sense. We were acculturated, for the most part. And, as we settled into that second and last year, one thing stood out to me: I understood what acculturation felt like. My peers accepted me. I knew the ropes and the routine. The odd sense of disorientation that had plagued me those first few months was over. I was "in." Knowing this gave me the freedom to be more myself, both in my classroom and in my relationships with my colleagues, and, as I would realize soon enough, my friends.

What I hadn't expected that second year was that Woody and I would no longer be the sole Americans in Zhezkazgan, and that I would react rather badly to this. There'd be two more Peace Corps volunteers in our little town, instead of just us.

I hadn't joined the Peace Corps to spend my time with Americans, I initially grumbled. But as I spent more time with them and began to enjoy the American company, conversation, and companionship, the two young women won me over.

Jessica worked at a medical cooperative doing human immunodeficiency virus (HIV) education. Thirty-something, she was vivacious and eager to make that difference we all hoped to make. Woody and I had first met her in May when she stayed with us for a week while she saw her future town, met her future coworkers, and found her future host family. Then she went back to Almaty to finish her Peace Corps training. She'd moved to Zhezkazgan over the summer while we were away.

I'd met our second volunteer, twenty-something Anna, while working at the Peace Corps' summer training. Posted to School #7, she'd arrive in November and live with Dina.

These were two dramatic changes from the training Woody and I had had: coming to their future site for a week of orientation before completing training; and, for the education volunteers, starting their year in November, rather than August. The changes made good sense, we thought.

Soon enough we four fell into a comfortable routine. The two women came to our place on Sunday mornings for Woody's pancakes-and-bacon breakfast, with real maple syrup, compliments of the regular care packages my mother sent. In between the casual chitchat and Peace Corps gossip, we'd plan our roles in the Thursday night English Club that Woody ran as his community project. I found their presence unexpectedly relaxing, our shared laughter intoxicating, and their initial disorientation validating.

The other big difference that second year was that the cultural differences that had so overwhelmed me faded into the background, and what was universally human stood out more easily. All cultures have rituals around play, marriage—at least about who gets to mate with whom—and death. Human beings, I believe, are born with an inherent need to feel loved, valued, and secure. Beyond wanting to survive, we all need to know where we belong. We also want to laugh, and we want to raise happy, healthy children who grow up to contribute to their world in some way.

And the differences in how each culture achieves these desires can be fascinating. Or frightening. It's all in one's perspective.

Woody's second year was a good one too. His teaching in particular became as enjoyable as he'd ever hoped. He taught "American Studies" with his new counterpart, Natasha, the vivacious red-haired denim-clad woman who'd welcomed me that first day with the huge bouquet of yellow flowers. He was having, he told me often, "great fun."

Though there were more textbooks at the university than I had at the college, Natasha had asked Woody at the end of the first year to find a book of short stories from which they could teach come fall.

Writing his own was the quickest way to get stories in front of the students and when Woody sat down over the summer to write them, out came *Jefferson, Connecticut: Stories of an Insecure Youth*, a collection of roughly autobiographical sketches set in the fictional town of Jefferson, Connecticut with made-up names. The Connecticut shoreline where he grew up and the underlying angst of the times, however, were clearly evident.

Natasha and another colleague created exercises in Russian for each story, and Zamzagul, their director, had the university publish it, excusing Woody from paying the customary fee that authors pay to have their books published in Kazakhstan.

But teaching these tales to the students presented a particular challenge.

"I want the students to focus on the stories," he told me. "If they knew these were my stories, they'd be too focused on me."

He believed this to such an extent that when a student asked him during class if the stories were about himself, he lied.

"There is a naiveté about my students," he explained to me one evening over dinner. "They have, after all, no experience reading literature. I get the feeling that reading and discussing themes in stories is all quite new for them." But Woody loved the challenge.

In my second year, I couldn't have been happier. I was a task-oriented grandmother teaching socially focused teenagers and young adults, a Western teacher in an Eastern classroom, a city girl living in a rural town, and I felt right at home. On my walk to school my first day back, a cow kept pace with me on the opposite sidewalk. After a few blocks, we arrived at the college at the same time.

"So long," I called out, as she continued. She ignored me. Somehow, along with all the other foreignness I'd adjusted to, walking to school with a cow now felt quite normal.

That I had no schedule for the coming semester was of no importance; it would come in its own time. Instead, two goals served as my rudder, fixing my course. I wanted my students and my colleagues to speak English more fluently, and I wanted them to know more of the wider world.

Helping them speak English was my Peace Corps job. To achieve that end, I wanted them to know that making mistakes is an important part of learning and that we can't fix anything if we keep it hidden. Fundamental to this, they had to know that however they did in my classroom, I was in their corner rooting for them.

Beyond that Peace Corps-mandated role, I wanted my colleagues and students to know more of the wider world. The Monday-night movies helped. But I hoped they might experience that wider world, not just see it on the screen.

The competitions I knew about from training—those that helped local Kazakhstanis go abroad—were geared to students and teachers in the elementary schools or universities, not the colleges. I needed to find foreign exchange programs for college teachers and students.

In my talks at the American Embassy in the spring, I'd learned about the Muskie Program, a perfect fit for Gulzhahan. But I still needed to find a program for my students. And as my second year began, this had me stymied.

Then, just as access to Saryarka for my English movie night project had fallen into my lap, so too came CCUSA, short for Camp Counselors USA. It came through Timur, the young man who had shaken my hand and thanked me after our first movie.

I'd added a post-movie discussion opportunity that second year, and Timur was the first to join Woody and me at the now familiar Cafe Aiya. But it turned out Timur didn't want to discuss the movie. He wanted to show us his pictures of New York City.

"I was in Times Square," he told us proudly, sitting over a late-night cup of *chai*. "I have photos." And he pulled out his collection of 4-by-6-inch black-and-whites and placed them on the table.

"How did you get to New York?" I asked, incredulous. He knew I didn't mean which airplane.

"CCUSA," he answered. "They sent me." And he regaled us with stories of being a camp counselor in New Jersey for two months, followed by two weeks' travel to see other parts of the USA. He chose New York City.

And so I found the program I'd been looking for. Sitting in a smoky café at nearly eleven o'clock at night, the contact information for the program I'd been searching for almost a year was handed to me, literally.

"How do I contact them?" I asked him, still expecting somehow to be disappointed. But Timur tore off a corner of his napkin and wrote down two web addresses and the cell number for Valeriy Nickolayevich, the director.

A quick search of the Internet at home and I learned that CCUSA was a California-based organization whose closest office to us was in Moscow. I called Valeriy the next day. He answered on the second ring, with excellent English touched with a heavy Russian accent.

He told me that students with at least one remaining year of study (i.e., my third-year students) could apply. They'd need to pay $3000—the amount that Gulsana had had—to cover their airfare and health insurance. The lucky students would get a summer job in the US that paid enough to recoup their initial outlay. It wasn't a job to make money. It was a job to help them experience the USA.

When Valeriy told me he'd come to Zhezkazgan in February to recruit, I realized I had just four months to identify which of my students should participate. It was just the sort of challenge I loved.

This year-long quest for my students to get to see the US was about to become a reality.

That last year I taught from what our Peace Corps Education Specialist liked to call "authentic materials."

I'd chosen three books: *Winnie-the-Pooh*, *Charlotte's Web*, and *Animal Farm*. I ordered every copy Amazon offered under $1 and had them mailed to my son David, who forwarded them to me. I also asked friends in the States to mail me additional copies.

My idea was that students would tackle these three books in their Home Reading class: *Winnie-the-Pooh* for the second-year students, *Charlotte's Web* for the third, and *Animal Farm* for the fourth and final-year students.

During this initial year, my team teachers and I would establish a lesson plan for each book, one they could continue to use after I was gone. Sustainability: that was another Peace Corps goal.

I wondered if my fourth-year students would be able to absorb the complexities in the *Animal Farm* story. Most, I knew, would only see the parable George Orwell constructed of life under Soviet rule as the simple story of farm animals taking over from an incompetent farmer. But, I hoped, a few might discover the political lessons Orwell intended: (1) that people often inherit the government they deserve, (2) that when their education is markedly weaker than that of their leaders, the public is lost, and (3) that blithely going along with those in power and assuming that they somehow know better is dangerous.

These were not the students who had asked me about Britney Spears and Michael Jackson. This particular group was made up of students who, after we had read the brief biography of Martin Luther King Jr., wrote their own "I Have a Dream" speech.

In their oral exams on *Animal Farm*, they made, with great felicity, appropriate connections between the various characters and Soviet rule. The deeper lessons, I could only hope, might occur to them as they grew older. I hadn't emphasized them in class because it seemed too overtly political. We simply read the book, planted the seed.

For now, I was content that I had introduced the book and that my students had synthesized what I'd put before them. I also felt unexpectedly humbled at the opportunity given me. These were, after all, lessons every society might remember from time to time. Mine included.

"There will be a hole in our heart when you go," Assem told me one afternoon in the teacher's lounge. "We will cry."

Assem and I had spent much time together since the day I'd first heard her say, "You American's ask 'Why?' all the time."

Over those two years, there had been two trips to Ulatau, a train trip to the 2006 NATEK convention, and visits to the local *banya*. I'd eaten meals in her home and we'd team-taught together.

Her simple comment had caught me by surprise and was the beginning of an important lesson for me. I'd noticed early on that "Why," seemed not to be in their vocabulary. But more than that, I began to wonder what was behind my insistence on knowing? *I so wanted to know.* It's a question that I continue to ask myself.

As my final year wound down, the thought of leaving these people I'd come to love, and with whom I felt fully accepted, saddened me. I would miss them terribly—their laughter, and their easy-to-be-with ways.

We'd worked hard to become this close. After the fiasco over the movies at Gulzhahan's house, about which I soon felt quite embarrassed, Assem had set my mind at peace.

"We learned a new word," she told me later. "Before you came, we never knew the word 'frustration.'" And she laughed, a laugh that never again bothered me.

Who would laugh with me when I got home? Woody has a broad smile and we chuckle at the same things, but his humor is subtle, dry. I've never seen him actually laugh, never mind giggle. I knew I would miss my life in Kazakhstan.

Yes, I'd cry, too, when the time came to leave.

I wondered, on occasion, if we should stay another year. Adding a third Peace Corps year was not unheard of. Rosa, at the college, had asked me to stay. They wouldn't get their new volunteer until November, and were worried, as I was, about those intervening months. I'm a homebody at heart and the truth was, right then, home for me was Zhezkazgan.

Woody, however, was eager to go home, and I wanted to be with my husband. The competing pulls were powerful.

Whoever said ambivalence means "one doesn't care" never felt true ambivalence. It could be my middle name. Ambivalent when I first came, proud to fulfill a long-held dream, curious about what we'd find, and at the same time terribly saddened and resentful for all I'd given up, and now ambivalent again at leaving.

Still, Zhezkazgan and these women I now called "my teachers" were in my soul.

"Anything I have accomplished here has been because of you," I told Gulzhahan one afternoon in my apartment. And she'd cried. Then I'd cried because she cried. We were a pair.

Chapter Nineteen
FAREWELL

Throughout the world and through the ages, seven is a significant number. We have seven days of creation, seven days of the week, seven deadly sins, Seven Wonders of the World, seven notes on our musical scale, and seven chakras of the body. In Islam there are seven heavens; in Kazakh lore, seven parts of the world, seven waters, seven saints, and seven treasures. And during our last full week in Zhezkazgan, there were seven farewell parties for Woody and me, each one filled with memories. I chose to believe this was a mere coincidence.

With our departure set for 11 pm, Friday night, June 2, what I aptly called "farewell week" kicked off in the college's Room 22. The classroom was a sea of bodies when I walked in, every chair filled and people standing up in the back and along the sides, a quick reminder there were no occupancy codes.

As Raikhan, one of my many top students in that year's English 39 class, introduced each class, the students came forward to offer me a reading, a poem, a performance, or a song. Asset, the tall young man I'd heard sing on my first Knowledge Day ceremony, sang in Kazakh. I knew he dreamed of being a Kazakh singer, and it sounded like he was well on his way, which was good, for he'd never earn his keep as an English teacher.

Following the student presentations, Bakhit (the administrator) gave me a pair of pierced earrings that matched a silver ring inlaid with black enamel that fit my middle finger perfectly.

"*S'paceba. Rakhmet*," I said, covering my thank-yous in both Russian and Kazakh. She beamed. I beamed too. The language was beginning to finally come automatically to me. *Now, that I'm leaving.*

On Sunday afternoon, our Tuesday night reading group took us on a *bon voyage* picnic. We met at a boathouse on the reservoir on the north end of town. In the two years we'd been there, we'd never known there was a boathouse on the reservoir.

The group had brought the fixings for a *shashlik* picnic: marinated meat kabobs and a metal grill to set over an open fire. I thought it a lovely gesture on such a hot day. But what I enjoyed most was watching this group work together, each one working as though they held picnics every week.

Monday night, farewell hugs and thank yous followed our final movie, *Norma Rae*.

Tuesday was a *bishparmak* dinner at Zhanara's apartment. Zhanara was a recent addition to our movie night advisory committee and a colleague of Togzhan's.

Wednesday, we ate *pelmini* at Tolganay's apartment with Assem and Gulzhahan, their husbands, and Gulzhan.

"There is more variety of food in America," I told them, curious what their reaction would be.

They picked up the challenge, each pressing their respective points. Gulzhahan, who had eaten with Woody and me in our apartment more often, agreed with me. The other three could not believe there could be more variety than a typical Kazakh *dastarkhan* with its multiple salads, candies, and other treats.

On they went, English quickly giving way to the more comfortable Kazakh, presenting their respective views, interspersed with much laughter. I loved listening to them, loved watching how animated they were, particularly when they disagreed. I tried breathing in the moment, for I believed I'd never know another quite like it.

Thursday's English Club party was a surprise. Woody and I had planned a pizza party, but we arrived to find that English 39's Raikhan had organized an evening of games, skits, songs, and a beautiful cake. We took our special seats from which to watch the evening's offerings.

Zhassik played a mournful tune he'd written for the occasion. He played it on his new guitar, the one Woody or I had been lugging around for two years. Then Woody borrowed it back and sang his favorite Leadbelly tune, *Leavin' Blues*. Together we sang Malvina Reynolds' *Sing Along*, a song about the importance of the group over the individual, whose chorus says, "For when we sing together, we'll be heard."

After the cake, the pizzas, the skits, and the songs, including dancing to The Village People's *YMCA*, an English Club favorite, Raikhan called Woody and me up to the front of the room. We stood together, unsure what to expect, as she tied a yellow ribbon around my neck and a brown one around Woody's, each the length of a Hawaiian lei. If this was some ancient Kazakh tradition, we'd never heard of it.

Then tiny Raikhan stepped back in front of me and slowly took a short strand of contrasting brown ribbon from a nearby basket and, as she tied it to my yellow necklace, she spoke. Her physical closeness added immeasurably to the intimacy of the moment and I listened in awe as she told me what my being there had meant to her, how I'd changed her life, and how she would miss me. Then she moved to Woody and tied a yellow ribbon onto his brown lei, murmuring words only he could hear. We would later learn that this was not an ancient Kazakh tradition. This was pure Raikhan.

Lines formed in front of us and as each person tied their small ribbon, he or she offered similar words of gratitude and affection. For over an hour, one by one, close to fifty people came up: my students, Woody's students, a few colleagues, and members of the community who had taken the time each week to improve their English—Larissa, who sold produce at the bazaar, Yerkian from the alcohol rehab hospital, and Christina, a schoolteacher who promised to see us that summer in the States when she would be a camp counselor in New Hampshire through CCUSA.

Our final farewell, Friday night, June 2, began at Assem's with my four teachers, our four husbands, and me. For our last meal, Assem made *galupsi* (stuffed cabbage). Assem is a good cook; not as good as Gulzhan but not as bad as Gulzhahan. This was a well-known fact and they all laughed when I actually said it aloud.

How comfortable we all were together. I knew I'd found my friends. Age was irrelevant; we shared experiences, memories now, and love. I still care deeply for these women whose lives I can't imagine living. They have endured more than I would ever want to and they continue to do so with grace, laughter, and true grit.

At nine o'clock, we walked *en masse* to the apartment Woody and I had called home for eighteen months. Our landlady met us one last time, to get my receipts for the utilities I'd paid and our keys, her keys now.

Our refrigerator had gone to Natasha, our stove to Assem, and a drop-leaf dining table that seated ten to Gulzhan. Our dishes and cookware had gone to Jessica, who would pass them down to the volunteer who followed. And our four-inch horsehair mattress went to Anna, who wanted it, with the caveat that she must also take my cross-country skis, which she didn't. (Probably because she knew I had never used them and she wouldn't either. Nor had the departing volunteer I'd gotten them from.)

Our luggage was packed and ready, considerably lighter than when we'd arrived. We were determined to have no overweight charges on our return flight. The apartment, now emptied of personal touches, echoed as we talked. And we talked for an hour before we had to leave for the train. Memories shared, stories retold, and laughter. There was always laughter. The hour passed quickly.

At ten o'clock, Zamzagul arrived with a minivan she'd arranged to cart us—and our luggage—to the station. I hadn't even thought about how we'd get there. Dina, Natasha, and Zamzagul's husband, Nariman, joined us outside our apartment along with Anna. Jessica had said her good-byes before she left for vacation. Natasha handed me a box of juice for the train.

Suddenly, Gulzhahan remembered some hard-boiled eggs she'd made for our trip and went home to get them, promising to meet us at the station. Darkhan, Assem, Tolganay, and Gulzhan went with Assem's husband in a car to the train station to see us off. *How nice*, I thought, *a dozen or so people there to see us off, just like our arrival.* But when we arrived at the station, we found such a crowd of faces waiting for us that I couldn't count them all.

Aniya, Woody's first counterpart, and her daughter were there. Everyone who had greeted us on our arrival was there once again to see us off—plus about forty others—except Gulzhahan. I searched for her tiny bobbing head, but didn't see it.

I still had Natasha's box of juice in my hand, but she and Dina had grabbed our food bags from the van and carried them for us. Our luggage went with the men, once again, and was stowed away in our *koopay* (passenger car compartment), the bigger pieces not to be thought of again until we arrived in Almaty.

Each person there wanted to say a personal good-bye. They shared good wishes, their hopes for our future. Strikingly, I heard no platitudes: no "see you later, take care" or "I hope to see you again." No one even promised to stay in touch.

How different this was from any significant good-bye I'd gone through before. How often we Americans blunt the impact of an impending loss by jumping to the future, planning a reunion, exchanging addresses.

That night, instead, I followed their lead and felt my loss. The reality hung over us all. Most of these young people would never leave Kazakhstan. Different constraints for different people: lack of money, pressing family obligations, or fear of the unknown. They said their good-byes with tears in their eyes and some of the strongest hugs I've ever had.

Then, as quickly as she'd disappeared, Gulzhahan was back, her bag of hard-boiled eggs somehow already on the train. She stood before me, her face bright red and wet from sobbing.

"I know we'll meet again. I don't know where or when, but we'll meet." I had to say it. I couldn't imagine it otherwise. Gulzhahan only nodded and continued to sob. She would make no promises.

The conductor had been calling for some time for us to board. Woody climbed up and into our *koopay* while I turned back for a final hug with my teachers. Then I climbed the stairs into the train, turned around, and let the full impact of this gathering hit me.

I pulled out my camera and took a photo. I knew I'd never forget the swarm of feelings I had at that moment. I didn't want to forget the faces either. This sea of energetic, grateful faces was the best possible gift. Their simple presence was all I needed, and I was grateful.

I turned and walked to my *koopay* to join my chocolates, my flowers, my juice, my luggage, and my husband. Woody and I sat facing each other next to the window as, right on time, 11:20 pm, our direct train to Almaty began to pull slowly out of the station.

I'd been overwhelmed so many times since we'd first arrived, and there it was again. For in that moment, I recognized fully that what I'd given up to be there had been worth it.

And, I also knew it was time to leave.

Chapter Twenty
BACK IN THE USA

The Peace Corps was right about our return home: it was not easy. The cab driver from the airport to our Philadelphia hotel was surly. Food portions were too large and plates too big.

We stepped over nonexistent doorsills for weeks. For months, we were surprised that we could understand conversations overheard; everyone spoke English. And for over a year we were uncomfortable drinking water straight from the tap.

During our first two months back, we toured the east coast of the United States and rediscovered humidity and the insects that go with it. Things that didn't exist before we left were now everyday features of American culture: Netflix, blogs, iTunes, text messaging, and colorful plastic shoes called Crocs.

But surely the hardest part of our return home was finding people interested in hearing of our experience. Our friends in Virginia, Frank and Rose, drove up to Chincoteague for dinner and heard our stories. We served *bishparmak*. But no one else seemed the least bit curious about other cultures, never mind the one with which we'd become so familiar. No one else asked to see our photographs, or even said, "Welcome home" until seven months later. To be fair, I'd written of my experiences in seventeen "email updates" to 108 of my "closest personal friends." Perhaps they'd heard enough.

Still, it was in some ways harder to come home than it had been to leave. That I hadn't expected, even though the Peace Corps explains this to all departing volunteers. Woody and I had assumed they were talking to the younger ones, those whose lives hadn't filled in, hadn't hardened into a form before they'd left. We expected to have a hard time adjusting there, and an easier time adjusting once we got home. So much for expectations, again.

We arrived home in time to catch the openings of Al Gore's penetrating film, *An Inconvenient Truth* and, at the insistence of the younger generation in my family, Sasha Baron Cohen's absurd *Borat: Cultural Learnings of America for Make Benefit Glorious Nation of Kazakhstan.*

From the sublime to the ridiculous.

NBC's *West Wing* had ended while we were away, and we could find nothing else to hold our attention. I felt repulsed by the various *Law & Order* spin offs and myriad *CSIs*. I shunned anything that showed the seamier side of life in America. I still do.

The news was filled with reports that left me feeling that greed had become a virtue while we were away. The seeds had been planted long ago, I knew, and we came home to the summer flowers and the harsh economic winter that would follow. TV, including the network news shows, which suddenly seemed more about entertainment, just didn't hold any appeal.

Alone on our nomadic summer, Woody and I found ourselves driving through Vermont, where we fell in love with thirty acres of woods in the Northeast Kingdom and a small stone house that stood upon it. Perhaps its very isolation made it so appealing after our disappointing return.

We moved there in the summer of 2007 and now raise ducks for the local slow food market, sing together in a hospice choir, enjoy our writers' group, and never take the lush and majestic landscape around us for granted.

My mother, whose very existence, according to Kazakh belief, keeps me young, moved in with us in 2008 and now has her own tiny cottage nearby. I have five grandchildren now, and they are a major part of my life, even though they are still too far away.

In a happy twist of fate, Merlin, our rescued greyhound, whom I thought I'd permanently lost, had three more years with us after we returned and is now buried in the woods behind our Vermont house.

His Philadelphia family had emailed me during our final December:

> *We are so happy to have cared for him and know how special he is. As sad as we will be to see him go, it makes my heart happy to know that he will be back with his first family who loves him dearly. I am assuming you will absolutely want him back, but certainly let me know if your thoughts have changed. Wishing you a very wonderful holiday season.*

I waited a week to respond. And when we picked him up, I never asked "why?" I only listened as she told me how he had bolted around their living room frantically in the minutes before I pulled into their driveway in a car Merlin had never known.

Since our return, two of my colleagues and two of my students have joined me in the States. Gulzhahan came first, in March of 2007, while we were still living in Chincoteague. The United States Embassy paid her way to present a poster session at a TESOL (Teachers of English to Speakers of Other Languages) convention in Seattle, Washington, and they extended her stay by ten days so we could visit. Woody picked her up in Washington DC and brought her to our home a few hours away.

"There are so many flags. Every place, I see American flags," she said when she saw me. I am now reminded of her every time I see an American flag waving, and that is quite often, as it turns out.

She and I drove to Cincinnati where my sons and their families were then living. "I saw the green grass in your movies," she told me *en route*. "But I always thought it was make-believe."

Gulzhan, my colleague and final Russian tutor, came to our home in Vermont in the summer of 2008 on a straightforward tourist visa, as the United States Consulate's Interim Director had suggested. I picked her up at Logan Airport in Boston and accompanied her a month later to New York City for a few days before she flew home from JFK Airport.

Her sense of humor had been hidden from me during my Peace Corps years, but in the intervening two years she'd been a counterpart to the Peace Corps volunteer who'd followed me, and her English had improved dramatically. My family rarely stopped laughing while she was with us.

None of my students or colleagues has yet to win any of the competitive awards that the Peace Corps focused on, though the teachers keep trying. Assem left the college to work at a local school just so she could apply for one of the grants for elementary teachers.

Gulzhahan, who now teaches at a university in Astana, stopped applying for the Muskie grant after three rejections and the birth of a second son. She is now focused on getting a Bolashak grant, funded by her government.

Two students from my second year's English 39 were able to visit us in 2008 through CCUSA. Raikhan lived with us and had a job at our local bed-and-breakfast, and then at a nearby camp. Nurken worked at a camp in Indiana and, when the season was over, joined us in Vermont.

Gulzhan, Raikhan, and Nurken were with us on my 60th birthday, complete with my sons, daughters-in-law, grandchildren, and mother. It was the closest I'd come to that large extended family I yearned for. We ate on long outdoor tables, like I'd seen in the movies, and I relished the moment, fully aware of what I had.

In the summer of 2009, in preparation for a second book on Kazakhstan, I returned to Zhezkazgan to talk with women who'd been stolen. Woody stayed home with our ducks and dog. It was the right decision for both of us. Gulzhan met me in Almaty and accompanied me on the train back to Zhezkazgan where I was a guest in her home. Gulzhahan joined us from Astana and together they played critical roles in finding the women for me to talk with and in interpreting during the interviews.

I saw many changes in Zhezkazgan during that visit. Among the more visible were the many "No Smoking" signs in the restaurants. I thought both of Zamzagul's "We'd never pass a law like that," and of my colleague's "Things here will never change," and felt hopeful. Small changes, yes, but changes nonetheless.

I Skype regularly with Gulzhahan and Gulzhan, and I use Facebook Messenger to chat with Assem and—more sporadically—Tolganay. I follow Kazakhstan in the news weekly through the Internet, and continue to learn all I can about her history. This I share on my website *www.janetgivens.com* as well as sharing on my blog many of the scenes that fell to the floor during the editing process.

Once settled in Vermont, Woody has continued with his singing, taking lessons for the first time in fifty years. He's joined two choruses and did a few gigs at local farmers markets. He's gone back to teaching, too—teaching phonetics and Introduction to Speech Pathology online.

My life also feels complete. I'm continuing to write and am taking the necessary steps to open a new psychotherapy practice. I'm excited by the prospect, but also know that it may never happen. I'm okay with that.

On those days when I find myself wanting "to know" or eager "to plan," I remember those two years in Kazakhstan, years in which I regularly, unknowingly, insulted or shocked someone, yet was nevertheless treated as a gift from God. Two years when I learned to laugh easily and often, and how to eat *bishparmak* with my five fingers.

Which brings me to perhaps my most important lesson. I have learned to live with not knowing. How often I've jumped off my high dives quickly, impatient to know what's next, eager to end the ambiguity.

I'm still jumping off high dives, and hopefully will for a long time to come. But thanks to my time in Kazakhstan, I wait a bit longer now, not knowing any better what lies below, but at least now able to take some time to enjoy the view.

To enjoy what is.

The End

Reviews are more important to authors today than ever before. If you enjoyed *At Home on the Kazakh Steppe*, please consider leaving a review at your favorite online retailer. Short reviews are just as valuable as long ones.

Thank you.

WANT MORE?

Check out Janet's Bonus Scenes collections at your preferred online distributor:

Fan Favorites:
Bonus Scenes from a Peace Corps Memoir
Published 2015

More Fan Favorites:
Bonus Scenes from a Peace Corps Memoir
Published 2016

ABOUT THE AUTHOR

Janet Givens was born in northern New Jersey at the beginning of the baby boomer generation. She has both a BS (NYU) and an MA (Kent State, OH) in sociology and worked in non-profit development for 25 years. She began her second career in 1999 as a Gestalt psychotherapist, which closed in 2004 when she began her Peace Corps journey.

Her first book, a textbook entitled *Stuttering* (Pro-Ed, Publisher), co-authored with C. W. Starkweather (now her husband) was the first textbook geared to people who stutter and the clinicians who treat them to read together. It was included in *Choice Magazine's* "Best Textbooks of 1997," a first in the speech pathology field.

Her second book, *At Home On the Kazakh Steppe: A Peace Corps Memoir*, won the Moritz Thomsen Peace Corps Experience

Award for 2015, presented annually for the best description of life in the Peace Corps. It has also won a coveted spot as a Kindle #1 Best Seller—for Russian Travel—and has been in the top ten for Biographies and Memoir/Travel and Adventure.

Currently, she shares her life with Woody Starkweather in the Green Mountains of Vermont, USA where, when she is not writing, she sings tenor in the local hospice choir, digs in the soil, or snowshoes somewhere on her 30 acres, edits her husband's latest novel, and enjoys being Grandma Janet to five little Buckeyes.

Oh yes, she loves that she is her dog Sasha's favorite human.

CONTACTS AND LINKS

Janet enjoys engaging with readers. Contact her
at any of these sites:

Email: givensj5112@yahoo.com

Website: janetgivens.com

Facebook Author Page: Janet.Givens.Author

Twitter: @GivensJanet

Pinterest: GivensJanet

Instagram: grammajanetKAZ15

ACKNOWLEDGMENTS

It takes a village to write a memoir. And my village is huge.

Seven years is a long time, and there were many iterations before it became *At Home on the Kazakh Steppe*. To those readers who read earlier versions, drafts, and excerpts I say, "I'm so sorry!" My book back then read like a doctoral dissertation, a series of journal entries, or a self-indulgent manifesto: pick one. But you gave me needed encouragement to keep going, and for that I also say, "Thank you."

To the members of the *Eastern Shore's Own* Tuesday night writers' group under Lenore Hart in Virginia and the members of the *End of the Road* Monday noon writers' group under Reeve Lindbergh in Vermont, I say, "Thanks for being there."

To Abby Colihan, MarySue Vinci, Susan Reed, Martha Holden, Lori Basher, Jeanne Shea, and Tara Ackerman I say, "Thank you for saying yes. That was very kind."

Jack Adler and Kelly Boyer Sagert led various *Writers' Digest* online workshops and helped me hone this craft in the genre now called Creative Nonfiction. From them I began to learn the difference between a memoir and a doctoral dissertation.

A special thanks to my first editor, Alison Stewart, who took the initial 435 pages to a more workable 325. Ginger Moran, Kelly Boyer Sagert, and Bonnie Lee Black also took professional stabs at it at one time or another and with each pass, the story became clearer and cleaner. I thank you.

Thanks to Nancy Drye, Megan Shulte, Annelies Lottman, Karen Huber, Amy Johnson, Denzel Benson, Jean Matray, Sarah Starkweather, and Mary-Elizabeth Briscoe, who read the full manuscript at one stage or another, sometimes twice, and always for free. I thank you for your time, your support, your good ideas and your friendship.

My final editor, Cami Ostman in Washington, kept her eye on that omnipresent "narrative arc" and held my hand as we slaughtered darling after darling, removing nearly one-third of my work. If the story reads smoothly and with dramatic tension, it's due to Cami's ability to combine ruthlessness with compassion. I am in awe. And I thank you.

Yes, it does take a village to do most anything, really. And here at home, as I brought my book to fruition, I turned to two old friends for help. Bob Thomas, *campbellthomas.com*, an architect and former neighbor of ours in Philadelphia, drew the fantastic map that helps us get oriented to the region. And Anne McKinsey, *amckwebandprint.com*, a graphic designer who once sang tenor with me, created my cover design. To both of them I am truly grateful. I encourage you to check their websites for more information on their various talents.

A huge thank-you to Victoria and Joe Twead, my publishers, aka Ant Press. Their unflagging enthusiasm for my book from the first read-through was a burst of fresh air on dying embers. And their diligent efforts to get my story launched into the world, while still leaving me in charge—or at least thinking I was—was masterful.

My final thanks goes to my husband, Woody Starkweather, who remains my first reader. For that, for your support over the last seven years as this book took shape, and for so very much more, I thank you. Joining the Peace Corps was your idea.

Acknowledgments for the 2015 Second Edition

My village continues to grow.

I add two new thank yous for help with this new edition. Sue Clamp steadfastly held my hand from her home in the UK, guiding me through the extensive maze that is Indie Publishing, particularly when I chose to self-publish at the same time as learning Scrivener. And, closer to home, fellow Vermonter Suzanne Rhodes helped me format the print book to meet Create Spaces' criteria. Thank you, Sue and Suzanne.

Acknowledgments for the 2015 Third Edition

Special thanks goes to Katherine Mayfield (*www.katherine-mayfield.com*) for proofreading help and for formatting the print version, and to Anne McKinsey (*www.amckwebandprint.com*) for enhancing the author bio picture.

Acknowledgments for the 2016 Fourth Edition

Sarah Starkweather (*www.starkediting.com*) made this fourth (and hopefully final) edition possible. Thank you, Sarah.

DISCUSSION QUESTIONS

1. Successful memoirs speak of universal truths. What are the universal truths expressed in the memoir *At Home on the Kazakh Steppe*?

2. In any story of middle-age change, there is a great deal of backstory that must be summarized or condensed. How do you feel the author handled the backstory?

3. What scene was most pivotal to the story? How was it pivotal?

4. What scene resonated most with you personally?

5. What is the significance of the title? Is there another title you might have chosen instead?

6. What surprised you the most about the book?

7. How did the characters change by the end of the book?

8. How did you find the excursions into Kazakh history, culture, politics, and geography?

9. Have your views or beliefs changed after reading this book?

10. What did you learn from this book?

11. Throughout the book, Janet declares her intent (her expectation) to eliminate expectations from her life. In your experience, is this possible?

12. What were the themes of *At Home on the Kazakh Steppe*? Were they adequately explored?

13. Have you lived in another culture? How did your experience compare?

Made in the USA
Monee, IL
24 April 2023

32402571R00152